P9-CBJ-206

Powell Lectures on Philosophy
at Indiana University

W. Harry Jellema, Editor

FIFTH SERIES

GOD AND PHILOSOPHY

WITHDRAWN

FIRST SERIES

THE LASTING ELEMENTS OF INDIVIDUALISM

WILLIAM ERNEST HOCKING

SECOND SERIES

IN THE SPIRIT OF WILLIAM JAMES

RALPH BARTON PERRY

THIRD SERIES

NATURALISM

JAMES BISSETT PRATT

FOURTH SERIES

WARS OF FAMILIES OF MINDS

WILLIAM LOWE BRYAN

FIFTH SERIES

GOD AND PHILOSOPHY

ÉTIENNE GILSON

GOD AND PHILOSOPHY

BY

ÉTIENNE GILSON

Published for Indiana University.

NEW HAVEN
YALE UNIVERSITY PRESS
London, Humphrey Milford, Oxford University Press.
1941

223.15
G42g

Copyright, 1941, by Yale University Press

Printed in the United States of America

All rights reserved. This book may not be reproduced, in whole or in part, in any form (except by reviewers for the public press), without written permission from the publishers.

NIHIL OBSTAT:

T. Lawrason Riggs,
Censor Deputatus.

IMPRIMATUR:

✠Maurice F. McAuliffe,
Episcopus Hartfordiensis.

March 15, 1941.

39952

THE
MAHLON POWELL FOUNDATION

MAHLON POWELL—1842–1928
WABASH, INDIANA

Extract from the last Will and Testament of Mahlon Powell:

Having entertained a desire for many years to assist in the cause of a higher education for the young men and women of our state and nation, and to that end provide a fund to be held in trust for the same, and to select a proper school or university where the same would continue in perpetuity, I will, devise and bequeath all of the real and personal property that I possess and of which I die seized to the Trustees of Indiana University, Bloomington, Indiana, to be held by them and their successors in office forever, the *Income* only to be used and applied in the support and maintenance of a *Chair* in *Philosophy* in said institution, and to be dedicated and forever known as "The Mahlon Powell Professorship in Philosophy" of said University.

In accordance with the provisions of this bequest, the Trustees of Indiana University have established a Chair in Philosophy on The Mahlon Powell Foundation. Each year a Visiting Professor will be invited to fill this Chair. The fifth lecturer on The Mahlon Powell Foundation is Étienne Gilson of the Pontifical Institute of Mediaeval Studies, Toronto.

HERMAN B WELLS
PRESIDENT, INDIANA UNIVERSITY

CONTENTS

	Preface	ix
I.	God and Greek Philosophy	1
II.	God and Christian Philosophy	38
III.	God and Modern Philosophy	74
IV.	God and Contemporary Thought	109
	Index	145

PREFACE

THESE four lectures deal with but one aspect of the highest of all metaphysical problems, and they deal with it on the basis of but a very limited number of historical facts, themselves rather taken for granted than technically established. The problem is the metaphysical problem of God. The particular aspect of this problem singled out for detailed examination is the relation which obtains between our notion of God and the demonstration of his existence. The approach to this philosophical question is the same as I have already presented in *The Unity of Philosophical Experience* (Scribner, New York, 1937) and in *Reason and Revelation in the Middle Ages* (Scribner, New York, 1938). It consists of extracting from the history of past philosophies the essential data that enter into the correct formulation of a philosophical problem, and of determining, in the light of such data, its correct solution.

This is by no means the only conceivable approach to philosophical truth. Neither is it a new one. Its incomparable models are to be found in several dialogues of Plato, for instance, in the *Theaetetus*, the *Philebus*, and the *Parmenides*. Aristotle has explicitly resorted to it, and successfully exploited it, in Book I of his *Metaphysics*. Naturally enough, it is attended by dangers of its own that arise from its very nature. First of all, it can deteriorate into a mere dialectical game wherein philosophical dogmas are debased into philosophical opinions, each of which is successively shown as true from its own point of view and as false from the viewpoint of any other one. The form of corruption proper to the philosophical method of the Academy is best exemplified by the Neo-Academy. But the same approach can also deteriorate into a history of the various philosophies taken as so many concrete, individual, and consequently irreducible facts. Now, while it is true that the history of philosophies is in itself a perfectly legitimate, and even a necessary, branch of historical learning, its very essence as history forbids it to aim at other than historical conclusions. Plato, Aristotle, Descartes, Kant have thought this and that on such and such philosophical questions. After ascertaining such facts, and making them intelligible by all the means at its disposal, the history of philosophies has exhausted its own program. But where it ends, philosophy can begin its own task, which is to judge the answers given to philosophical problems by Plato, Aristotle, Descartes, and Kant in the light of the necessary data of these problems themselves. The historical approach to philosophy uses the history of philosophies as a handmaid to philosophy.

Like everything else, this can be well done or

badly done. Of all the bad ways to do it, the worst is probably that of some textbooks of dogmatic philosophy, in which a certain doctrine, posited as true, is used as a criterion to determine automatically the truth or falsity of all others. There is but one order of knowledge where such a method legitimately applies, and that is revealed theology. If we believe by faith that God has spoken, since what God says is true, all that contradicts the word of God can, and must, be at once excluded as false. The familiar formula of Saint Thomas Aquinas, *Per hoc autem excluditur error*, is a perfect expression of such a theological attitude. But this formula cannot be transferred from theology to philosophy unless it first receive some qualification. The word of God excludes all contrary errors because, *qua* word of God, the word of God is true. The word of no philosopher, on the contrary, can exclude contrary statements as false, because the word of no philosopher is true *qua* the word of this philosopher. If what he says is true, what excludes all contrary errors is that which makes what he says true, namely, his success both in correctly posing a certain problem and in doing justice to all the data required for its solution. If, in the following pages, Thomas Aquinas appears a bit too much like the *deus ex machina* of some abstract metaphysical drama, the ready objection will be that I have spoken as a Thomist, measuring all the other philosophies by the yardstick of Thomism. I beg at least to assure my readers that if I have done this—which is but too possible—I have committed what appears to me personally as the one unforgivable sin against the very essence of philosophy. Yet, before condemning me for such a crime, they will have to make sure that I have actually committed it.

I was educated in a French Catholic college, which I left, after seven years of studies, without having heard even once, at least as far as I remember, the name of Saint Thomas Aquinas. When the time came for me to study philosophy I went to a state-controlled college, whose professor of philosophy, a belated disciple of Victor Cousin, had certainly never read a line of Thomas Aquinas. At the Sorbonne, no one of my professors knew anything about his doctrine. All that I learned concerning it was that, were anyone enough of a fool to read it, he would find there an expression of that Scholasticism which, since the time of Descartes, had become a mere piece of mental archeology. To me, however, philosophy was neither Descartes nor even Kant; it was Bergson, the genius whose lectures still remain in my memory as so many hours of intellectual transfiguration. Henri Bergson is the only living master in philosophy I have ever had, and I consider it as one of the greatest blessings bestowed by God on my philosophical life that, owing to Bergson, I have met philosophical genius both somewhere else and otherwise than in books. Yet, even though Bergson says that, ever since his earliest philosophical efforts, he has always been on his way toward the God of the Jewish-Christian tradition, he himself did not at that time know it; at any rate, nobody has ever been led by Bergson to the philosophical method of Saint Thomas Aquinas.

The man to whom I am indebted for my first knowledge of Saint Thomas was a Jew. He had never opened a single one of the works of Thomas, nor did he intend ever to do so. But he was, besides many other good things, a man of an almost uncanny intelligence, with a surprising gift of seeing facts in an impartial, cold, and objective light, just as they were. As soon as I had attended the course of lectures in Hume he was then giving at the Sorbonne, I realized that, to me, to understand any philosophy would always mean to approach it as I had seen Lucien Lévy-Bruhl approach that of Hume. When, two years later, I went to him for a subject of a thesis, he advised me to study the vocabulary and, eventually, the matter borrowed from Scholasticism by Descartes. Hence the book which I have since published under the title: *La Liberté chez Descartes et la théologie.* Historically speaking, this work is now out of date, but its nine long years of preparation taught me two things: first, to read Saint Thomas Aquinas; secondly, that Descartes had vainly tried to solve, by means of his own famous method, philosophical problems whose only correct position and solution were inseparable from the method of Saint Thomas Aquinas. In other words (and my surprise can still be found naïvely expressed in the last pages of that now old book), I discovered that the only context in which the metaphysical conclusions of Descartes made sense was the metaphysics of Saint Thomas Aquinas.

To say that this came to me as a shock would be unduly to dramatize what was but the objective conclusion of patient historical observations. Since, however, it had become clear to me that, technically speaking, the metaphysics of Descartes had largely been a clumsy overhauling of scholastic metaphysics, I decided to learn metaphysics from those who had really known it, namely, those very Schoolmen whom my own professors of philosophy felt the more free to despise as they had never read them. Their study has wholly convinced me, not at all that to philosophize consists in repeating what they have said, but rather that no philosophical progress will ever be possible unless we first learn to know what they knew. The chaotic condition of contemporary philosophy, with the ensuing moral, social, political, and pedagogical chaos, is not due to any lack of philosophical insight among modern thinkers; it simply follows from the fact that we have lost our way because we have lost the knowledge of some fundamental principles which, since they are true, are the only ones on which, today as well as in Plato's own day, any philosophical knowledge worthy of the name can possibly be established. If anybody be afraid of sterilizing his own precious philosophical personality by simply learning how to think, let him read the books of Jacques Maritain as a sedative for his fears of intellectual barrenness. The great curse of modern philosophy is the almost universally prevailing rebellion against intellectual self-discipline. Where loose thinking obtains, truth cannot possibly be grasped, whence the conclusion naturally follows that there is no truth.

The following lectures rest on the contrary assumption that truth can be found, even in metaphysics. They do not contain anything like a history of the philosophical problem of God; important doctrines have been barely sketched, while innumerable others have not been mentioned at all. Neither do they pretend to be a sufficient demonstration of the existence of God. Their aim and scope are rather to achieve the clear and precise determination of a certain metaphysical problem. I would like to think that, after reading them, some among my readers will at least understand the meaning of their own words, when they say that the existence of God cannot be demonstrated. Nobody really knows that this cannot be done unless he realizes at least what it would be to do it. The only philosopher who has made me clearly realize the full metaphysical implications of this problem is Saint Thomas Aquinas. I am as fond of my own intellectual freedom as anyone else, but I want to be free to agree with somebody when I think that what he says is right. Saint Thomas Aquinas never thought of anything like a "Thomistic truth." These words do not even make sense. Judging various answers to the problem of God on the ground of their relative aptness to do justice to all its demands, I have come to the conclusion that the best answer to it has been given by the man who, because he was the first to grasp the deepest implications of this problem, has also been the first freely to bow to the metaphysical necessity of its only solution. Anybody who can is still today welcome to do the same thing as freely as Thomas Aquinas himself ever did it. As to him who either cannot or will not do it, let him have at least the satisfaction of turning down the only pertinent solution to a true problem: not the supreme carpenter of Paley or the supreme watchmaker of Voltaire, but the infinite act of self-existence, by whom all the rest is, and as compared with whom all the rest is as though it were not.

I would like to express my gratitude to the Board of Trustees of Indiana University which approved my appointment as Visiting Professor of Philosophy on the Mahlon Powell Foundation, for 1939–40. I will perhaps be permitted to say how particularly grateful I feel to the members of the department of Philosophy of Indiana University for so graciously welcoming me at a time when men of different nations feel little inclination unreservedly to trust one another. But I must quite especially thank Professor W. Harry Jellema. His letter of invitation so clearly outlined and defined for me the task I was desired to undertake, that to quote one of its sentences remains perhaps my best chance, if not to justify the contents of these lectures, at least to make clear their general intention: "For too many philosophers today, philosophy no longer means anything of what it ought to mean; and for almost all our contemporaries Christianity has nothing to say which science has not disproved, nor anything intellectually respectable which had not already been said by the Greeks." It has been my intention to show, on the particular problem of God, that the Christian philosophers have said, owing to the Greeks, things that had never been said by the Greeks themselves; that these things are so intellectually respectable that they have become part and parcel of modern philosophy; and that, though no one can expect science to prove them, we should not mistakenly accept as their disproval by science the failure of some scientists to understand the fundamental problems of metaphysics.

These lectures are printed exactly as they were read at Indiana University and as they were written at the Pontifical Institute of Mediaeval Studies, Toronto. It is an uncommon blessing to live in such a place, where friends patiently suffer one to try on them his provisorily last ideas about any and every question. To the name of the Rev. G. B. Phelan, President of the Pontifical Institute of Mediaeval Studies, who never failed to help me through my philosophical adventures, I must this time add the name of my eminent friend Professor Jacques Maritain. To both of them I feel deeply indebted for confirmations, suggestions, and corrections, which, I am sure, have made this little book a little less unworthy of its subject.

ÉTIENNE GILSON

Pontifical Institute of Mediaeval Studies

GOD AND PHILOSOPHY

I

GOD AND GREEK PHILOSOPHY

IN the history of Western culture, every chapter begins with the Greeks. This is true of logic, of science, of art, of politics, and it is equally true of natural theology; but it is not at once clear where one should look, in the past of ancient Greece, for the origins of our philosophical notion of God.

As soon as we read the texts of Aristotle whence most of our information concerning early Greek philosophy is derived, the difficulty appears in full. Speaking of Thales the Milesian, Aristotle says that, according to this philosopher, the first principle, or element, or substance, of which all things are born and to which all things ultimately return, is water. To which Aristotle adds, in another text, that according to the same Thales "all things are full of gods."[1] How can these two distinct statements be philosophically reconciled?

A first way to do it is to identify the two notions of water and of divinity. This is what a modern scholar has done by making Thales

1. Aristotle, *Metaphysics,* I, 3, 983b, 20–27; *De Anima,* I, 5, 411a, 8.

say that water is not only a god but the supreme god. In such an interpretation of the texts, "the supreme god, and the cosmogenetic god, are one divine power, Water."[2] The only difficulty in accepting this simple and logical solution of the problem is that it ascribes to Thales several ideas which he may very well have held, but of which Aristotle says absolutely nothing.[3] According to the earliest testimonies at our disposal, Thales did not say that water was a god, or that, among the gods which crowd this world, there was a supreme god; consequently he has not said that water

2. R. Kenneth Hack, *God in Greek Philosophy to the Time of Socrates* (Princeton University Press, 1931), p. 42.

3. Aristotle has nowhere reconstructed the thought of Thales along the lines followed by modern scholars. In his *De Anima,* I, 5, 411a, 7, he relates as another opinion of Thales that the magnet has a soul, since it is able to move iron; whence Aristotle himself infers, obviously as a conjecture, that Thales' statement "all things are full of gods" had perhaps been inspired by the opinion that "soul is diffused throughout the whole universe." For an English translation of the texts related to Thales, see Milton C. Nahm, *Selections from Early Greek Philosophy* (F. S. Crofts, New York, 1930), pp. 59–62. After Aristotle, and chiefly under Stoic influences, the doctrine of the world-soul was ascribed to Thales, until Cicero (*De Nat. Deorum,* I, 25) completed the circle by identifying the so-called world-soul of Thales with God. Cf. John Burnet, *Early Greek Philosophy* (4th ed. London, A. and C. Black, 1930), pp. 49–50. All this is a later reconstruction of the doctrine of Thales, and there is no authentic historical evidence to support it.

was the supreme god. Here, in a nutshell, is what is to remain for us the whole problem. On the one side, a man posits a certain natural element as the very stuff this world is made of. Let us call it water, but the name does not make any difference, and the problem will remain identically the same when the first principle is called fire, air, the Indeterminate, or even the Good. On the other side, the same man posits as a sort of axiom that all things are full of gods. Whence our own immediate conclusion that, to him, water is not only one of the gods, but the greatest of all. Yet the more logical such an inference appears to us, the more surprising it should seem that this man himself did not think of drawing it. There is at least an off chance that, were he now confronted by us with our own inference, he might object to it as to an illegitimate one. In short, instead of writing the history of philosophy as it has been, we write the history of what philosophy should have been. A very bad way to write the history of philosophy indeed, and, as will soon be seen, a sure way to miss its deepest philosophical meaning.

Another method to get rid of our difficulty is, instead of turning water into a god, to turn the god of Thales into water. This was exactly the purpose John Burnet had in mind when he advised his readers not "to make too much of the saying that all things are full of gods."[4] What lies behind Burnet's advice is his absolute conviction that "there is no trace of theological speculation" either in Thales the Milesian or in his immediate successors. In other words, when Thales says that the world is full of gods, he does not really means "gods." He simply means some physical and purely natural energy, such as water, for instance, which, according to his own doctrine, is the first principle of all things. The same observation should apply to the successors of Thales. When Anaximander says that his own first principle, the Indeterminate, is divine, or when Anaximenes teaches that infinite air is the first cause of all that is, including gods and divine beings, they do not think of the gods as possible objects of worship. In Burnet's own words, "this non-religious use of the word *god* is characteristic of the whole period" of early Greek philosophy,[5] to which my only objection is that very few words have a more distinctly religious connotation than the word "god." Everybody is welcome to interpret the

4. J. Burnet, *op. cit.*, p. 50.

5. *Ibid.*, pp. 13, 14, and 50. Burnet's rationalistic interpretation of early Greek philosophy is itself a reaction against the sociological interpretation of it developed in F. C. Cornford, *From Religion to Philosophy* (London,

sentence, "All things are full of gods," as meaning that there is not a single god in anything, but the least that can be said of it is that it is a rather bold interpretation.

Instead of making Thales say either that his gods are but water or that his water is a god, why not try this third historical hypothesis, namely, that as a rule philosophers mean to say just what they do say? It is a risky business to teach Greek to a Greek. Were we asked what were the exact connotations of the word "god" in a Greek mind of the fifth century B.C., I would at once admit that this is a very difficult question to answer. Yet we might try, and the best way for us to do it would probably be to read first the works in which the origin, the nature, and the functions of what the Greeks called the "gods" have been described at some length. There is Homer, for instance, and there is Hesiod. And I know full well that, even concerning Homer himself, it has been maintained that where he says "god" he does not mean "god." But surely there is no harm in our asking him what he does mean; and before turning down his

1912). Burnet does not want us "to fall into the error of deriving science from mythology" (*op. cit.*, p. 14). In which, as I think, Burnet is right, but if it is a mistake to derive Thales' science from mythology, it is another mistake to eliminate mythology from Thales' science.

answer, we should at least give it all due consideration.[6]

The first striking fact about the Greek meaning of this word is that its origin is not a philosophical one. When the early Greek philosophers began to speculate, the gods were already there, and the philosophers merely inherited them from those men whom all antiquity, up to the time of Saint Augustine, has called the Theologian Poets. To limit ourselves to Homer's *Iliad*, the word "god" there seems to apply to an incredible variety of different objects. A Greek god could be conceived as what we ourselves would call a person, as happened in the case of Zeus, Hera, Apollo, Pallas Athena, in short, of all the so-called Olympians. But the god could just as well be some physical reality, such as, for instance, the great god Ocean, or the Earth itself, or the Sky. When, at the beginning of the *Iliad*, XX, Zeus bade Themis call the gods to council, "there was no River came not up,

6. On the position of Wilamowitz, Rohde, and Edward Meyer, see the judicious remarks of R. K. Hack, *op. cit.*, pp. 4–6. Homer has been considered by some of his modern interpreters as being not only irreligious, but even antireligious. According to some others, on the contrary, he was a religious reformer and, so to speak, the Saint Paul of early Greek paganism. Such is, for instance, the position of Gilbert Murray, *Five Stages of Greek Religion* (New York, Columbia University Press, 1925), p. 82.

save only Ocean, nor any Nymph, of all that haunt fair thickets and springs of rivers and grassy water meadows."[7] Nor is this all. Even the great natural fatalities which govern all mortal lives appear to us in Homer's *Iliad* as so many gods. Such are Terror, Rout, and Strife; and such also are Death, and Sleep, the lord of gods and men, who is the brother of Death.

At first sight, it does not seem easy to find common elements in this heterogeneous medley of beings, of things, and even of mere abstractions. On closer inspection, however, there appears at least one. Whatever the real nature of what they designate, these names of gods all point to living powers, or forces, endowed with a will of their own, operating in human

7. *Homeri Ilias,* ed. Thomas W. Allen (Oxford, Clarendon Press, 1931), 3 vols. The verse will be quoted from this edition; but the texts will be quoted from *The Iliad of Homer,* trans. by A. Lang, W. Leaf, and Ernest Myers (New York), The Modern Library. Cf. Bk. XX, vv. 7–9, p. 368. It is noteworthy that even the personal Greek gods seem to have originally been but personalized natural forces—Zeus, G. Murray says, "is the Achaean sky-god," Phoebus Apollo "is a sun-god," Pallas Athena is "the Dawn-goddess, Eos," associated with Athens (*op. cit.,* pp. 71–74). On the psychological problems raised by this personalizing process, see the always suggestive and penetrating remarks of R. K. Hack, *op. cit.,* pp. 12–16. On Greek religious life and feelings, see A. J. Festugière, *L'Idéal religieux des Grecs et l'Évangile* (Paris, Gabalda, 1932), pp. 20–32.

lives and swaying human destinies from above. The popular pinkish picture of Ancient Greece as the seat of an intelligent race leading a carefree life in the peaceful enjoyment of a friendly nature and under the guidance of good-natured gods does not agree too well with what we learn from the Greek epics, from the Greek tragedies, or even from the political history of Greece. At any rate it is wholly at variance with what is known of Greek religion. A religious-minded Greek felt himself an instrument in the hands of innumerable divine powers to which not only his acts but even his thoughts were ultimately submitted. As everybody knows, from its very first verses the subject of Homer's *Iliad* is the wrath of Achilles and the disasters it brought on the Greeks. Now the cause for the wrath of Achilles was his unjust treatment by King Agamemnon. As to the cause of this unjust treatment, Agamemnon himself tells us what it was: "It is not I who am the cause, but Zeus, and Erynis that walketh in the darkness, who put into my soul fierce madness on the day when in the assembly I, even I, bereft Achilles of his meed. What could I do? It is god who accomplisheth all."[8]

8. Cf. Homer, *Iliad,* Bk. XIX, vv. 86–90, English trans., p. 357. This point is later on confirmed by Achilles him-

The first characteristic of these divine powers is life. Whatever else he may happen to be, a Greek god never is an inanimate thing; he is a living being, just as men themselves are, with the sole difference that whereas human life is bound sometime to come to an end, the Greek gods never die. Hence their other name: the Immortals.[9] And the second characteristic of these Immortals is that all of them are related much more to man than to the world at large. Let us take, almost at random, any one of those permanent fatalities that sway the lives of men; it is a god. Such are Earth, Sky, Ocean; all the Rivers which bring life to man by fecundating his fields or threaten him with death by overflowing their banks; such also are Sleep and Death, Fear and Strife, implacable Vengeance, and Rout, and Rumor who is the Messenger of Zeus. But we should

self: "Father Zeus, sore madness dealest thou verily to men. Never could the son of Atreus (i.e. Agamemnon) have stirred the soul within my breast, nor led off the damsel (i.e. Briseis) implacably against my will, had not Zeus willed that on many of the Achaians death should come" (Bk. XIX, vv. 270–274, English trans., p. 362). Every Greek poem, like every Greek tragedy, presupposes a "Prelude in Heaven" which gives the poem, or the tragedy, its full meaning.

9. The two notions of life and of blood are inseparable in a Greek mind. Since the Greek gods have no blood, they cannot lose it, and consequently they cannot die. Cf. *Iliad,* Bk. V, vv. 339–342, English trans., p. 84.

not forget, after the dreadful divinities, the benevolent ones: Justice, Love, and the Muses, and the Graces; in short, all the immortally living powers which rule the lives of mortal men.

To these two characteristics let us add still a third one. A divine power that reigns supreme in its own order may have to yield, on some definite points, to other gods equally supreme in their own order. For instance, although the Immortals never die, they sleep; Sleep then is "the lord of all gods and of all men."[10] This is a universal law. Just as they sleep, the Immortals love and desire; hence the words of the goddess Hera to Aphrodite: "Give me now Love and Desire wherewith thou overcomest all the Immortals, and mortal men." Hera, the only divinity whom Zeus is really afraid of, whom he seldom sees without feeling "sore troubled" because "she upbraideth him ever amid the immortal gods"; in short, the most powerful divinity by whom any man's life can be swayed, his wife.

Yet, the only absolute power to which Zeus himself is submitted does not rule him from without but from within. It is his own will. The greatest of all gods, the father of gods

10. *Ibid.*, Bk. XIV, v. 233, English trans., pp. 256–257.

and men, the god of counsel, Zeus himself remains powerless before his own consent, once given.[11] And Zeus cannot but consent to his own will, though his will is by no means identical with his own individual preference. What is the deeper will of the deeper Zeus is that everything may happen according to Fate and to Destiny. When his most beloved son Sarpedon is engaged in fight against Patroklos, Zeus knows it is fated that Sarpedon should die. Torn between his fatherly love and his consent to Fate, Zeus at first hesitates; but Hera sternly reminds him of his duty: "A mortal man long doomed to fate dost thou desire to deliver again from death of evil name? Work thy will, but all we other gods will in no way praise thee." Thus spoke Hera, "nor did the father of gods and men disregard her. But he shed bloody raindrops on the earth, honouring his dear son, that Patroklos was about to slay."[12] Because the deeper will of Zeus is one with the invincible power of Fate, Zeus is the most powerful of all the gods.

If this be true, the definition of a Greek god should run thus: a god, to any living

11. *Ibid.*, Bk. I, vv. 524–527, English trans., p. 16: "No word of mine is revocable nor false nor unfulfilled when the bowing of my head hath pledged it."

12. *Ibid.*, Bk. XVI, vv. 439–461, English trans., p. 302.

being, is any other living being whom he knows as lording it over his own life. That what happens to a being endowed with life can be explained but by another being also endowed with life, was to the Greeks a point beyond discussion, and the fact that they felt sure of it should be to us a strong reminder not to speak lightly of Greek religion, or of the Greek gods. A religious-minded Greek felt himself the passive battlefield of overpowering and too often mutually conflicting divine influences. His will was at their mercy. As Pindar says: "From the gods come all the means of mortal exploits; thanks to the gods are men wise and brave and eloquent."[13] But the reverse is equally true. The same heroes whom we see bravely fighting so long as the gods are with them shamelessly take to their heels as soon as the same gods desert them. They then feel what they call "the turning of the sacred scales of Zeus"; as to Zeus himself, he knows this turning of the scales because he sees it happening within his own hands: "When the fourth time Hector and Achilles had reached the springs, then the Father hung his golden balances, and set therein two lots of dreary death, one of Achilles, one of horse-taming

13. Pindar, *Pythian Odes,* I, vv. 41–42, ed. J. Sandys (London, 1915), p. 159. Loeb Classical Library.

Hector, and held them by the midst, and poised. Then Hector's fated day sank down, and fell to the house of Hades, and Phoebus Apollo left him."[14] Once more the will of Zeus is reduced to his consent to Destiny; consequently, Hector must die. A world where everything came to men from without, including their feelings and passions, their virtues and their vices, such was the Greek religious world. The immortal beings from whose favor, and disfavor, everything thus came to men—such were the gods of the Greeks.

We are now beginning to realize why it was not so easy for a Greek philosopher to deify his first universal principle of all things. The question is not to know if Thales, Anaximenes, and their successors still believed in the gods of Homer, or if, rather, they had not already begun to eliminate most of them as being mere fabulous imaginings. Granting that this second hypothesis is more likely to be true than the first one, the difficulty remains the same so long as the notion of god still retains something of its religious connotations. If, speaking as a philosopher, you say that everything is x, and that x is a god, you are thereby saying that everything is not only a god but the same god. How then could you add that the

14. *Iliad,* Bk. XXII, vv. 208–213, English trans., p. 406.

world is full of *gods?* If, speaking as a religious man, you begin by positing that the world is full of gods, either your gods are not the principles of those things in which they are, or else, if each god is such a principle, it can no longer be said that there is but one principle of all things. Since Thales and his successors were speaking as philosophers, their only logical choice was the first one. They should have said that everything was but one and the same god, thus reaching at once the very same materialistic pantheism of the Stoics wherewith Greek philosophy was ultimately to end. Abstractly speaking, the early Greek philosophers could have immediately brought the evolution of Greek natural theology to its close; but they did not, because they did not want to lose their gods.[15]

15. The continuity of the religious and philosophical Greek thought about God is, on the contrary, strongly emphasized by R. K. Hack, *op. cit.*, p. 39. We are thus confronted with two antinomic interpretations of the same texts. According to Burnet, when Thales says that "all things are full of gods," he does not really mean "gods." According to R. K. Hack, the authentic thought of Thales is that "water is the living and divine substance of the universe" (*ibid.*). In point of fact, in the text of Aristotle which is the main source of our knowledge of Thales, mention is made of the similar doctrine of "the first students of the gods" concerning Ocean and Thetys considered as "parents of generation"; after which Aristotle adds: "Whether there is such ancient and early opinion concerning nature would be an obscure

Our first reaction is naturally to blame such a lack of philosophical courage; but there may be less courage in following abstract logic than in refusing to let it play havoc with the manifold of reality. When a philosopher asks himself "What stuff is the world made of?" he is asking a purely objective and impersonal question. When, on the contrary, Agamemnon declares: "What could I do? It is god who accomplisheth all," he is answering this most subjective and personal problem: What has made me act as I did? Now it is not at once evident that correctly to

question; but Thales is said to have expressed this opinion in regard to the first cause." *Metaphysics,* I, 3, 983b, 18–984a, 2; M. C. Nahm, *op. cit.,* pp. 60–61. It is therefore clear that Aristotle had no certitude concerning the continuity of the two doctrines. To blame him for having failed "to include the attribute of divinity along with the Psyche that is diffused through all things" (R. K. Hack, *op. cit.,* p. 42, n.), is also to take it for granted that Aristotle should have done so, which is by no means proved. To conclude, Burnet links together these two statements, "All things are full of gods," "The magnet is alive" (*op. cit.,* p. 48), so as to suggest that, to Thales, the gods are physical forces of the same sort as the magnet; R. K. Hack links together the two statements: "All things are full of gods," and "There is a soul diffused through all things," so as to suggest that the world-soul is God. Aristotle, on the contrary, has never linked together any two of these various theses, and has not even explicitly ascribed the doctrine of the world-soul to Thales (*De Anima,* I, 5, 411a, 7–9). The fact that some scholars eliminate god from texts where god is, does not authorize us to put god in texts where god is not.

answer the first problem is also to solve the second one. We might well try to quench Agamemnon's curiosity by telling him that, since everything is water, the reason why he has bereft Achilles of his meed must have had something to do with water. I think he would listen to our explanation, but we may be sure that by the word "water" he would at once understand the god Ocean; to which his ready objection would surely be that our answer is the wrong answer because our god is the wrong god. Not Okeanos, King Agamemnon would say, but Blind Folly (Ate) is the only conceivable cause for such mad behavior on my part.[16] Blind Folly is a god; water is but a thing.

When Greek philosophers themselves used the word "god," they too had in mind a cause which was more than a mere thing, whence for them the difficulty of finding for the problem of the world order a single and all-comprehensive solution. As philosophers, even the very first Greek thinkers appear to us as perfect representatives of a truly scientific attitude of mind. To them reality was essentially what they could touch and see, and their fundamental question about it was: What is it? To the question: What is the Ocean? the an-

16. *Iliad,* Bk. XIX, vv. 91–92, p. 357.

swer, He is a god, simply does not make sense.[17] Conversely, to the question: What is the world? the formula, "All things are full of gods," cannot possibly do for an answer. Taking the world as a given reality, the Greek philosophers simply asked themselves what its "nature" was, that is, what was the essential substance of all things and the hidden principle of all their operations? Was it water, or air, or fire, or the Indeterminate? Or was it perhaps a mind, a thought, an Idea, a law? Whatever answer they might give to their problem, the Greek philosophers always found themselves confronted with nature as with a self-explaining fact. "Nothing can come into being from that which is not," Demokritos says, "nor pass away into that which is not."[18] Had it been possible for nature not to be, it would have never existed. Now nature is there; hence it has always been there, and ever shall be. So necessary and eternal was a

17. This is true of even the theogony of Hesiod (cf. R. K. Hack, *op. cit.,* chap. iii, pp. 23–32). Much more systematic than that of Homer, the hesiodic *Theogony* still essentially remains a theology, that is to say, a religious explanation of the world by means of certain persons, not a philosophical explanation of the world by means of one or several natural things. Mythology is religion, philosophy is knowledge, and although true religion and true knowledge ultimately agree, they represent two distinct types of problems, demonstration and solutions.

18. Text in M. C. Nahm, *op. cit.,* p. 165, n. 44.

nature thus understood, that when a Greek philosopher found himself driven to the conclusion that this world of ours must have had a beginning and is destined some day to reach its end, he would immediately conceive both the beginning and the end of this world as but two moments in an eternal cycle of ever-recurring events. As Simplicius says: "Those who assumed innumerable worlds, for instance Anaximander, Leukippos, Demokritos and, at a later date, Epicurus, held that they came into being and passed away *ad infinitum*, some always coming into being and others passing away."[19] If this cannot be considered as a scientifically proved answer to the problem of nature, it is at least the adequate philosophical expression of what an exhaustive scientific explanation of the world of nature should be. This type of explanation falls short where it takes itself for an answer to the specifically distinct problems of religion.

Whether such scientifically unanswerable problems should be asked or not is a legitimate question, but it is not our present question.

19. Cf. J. Burnet, *op. cit.*, p. 59. Concerning Anaximander, see texts in M. C. Nahm, *op. cit.*, pp. 62, 63; on Leukippos and Demokritos, *op. cit.*, pp. 160–161, or J. Burnet, *op. cit.*, pp. 338–339. The best work on this question is that of A. Dies, *Le Cycle mystique* (Paris, F. Alean, 1909).

We are now dealing with historical facts. Now one of these facts is that the Greeks themselves have constantly raised specifically religious problems; another one is that they have given these problems specifically religious answers; and it is a third fact that the greatest among the Greek philosophers have found it very hard, not to say impossible, to reconcile their religious interpretation of the world with its philosophical interpretation.

The only element common to their two views of nature was a sort of general feeling that, for whatever reason things may be happening, that which is happening could not possibly not happen. Hence the often-propounded view of the history of Greek philosophy, which shows it as a progressive rationalization of primitive Greek religion. Yet there are difficulties. The religious notions of Fate and Destiny are specifically distinct from the philosophical notion of necessity. That all men, including Hector, must ultimately die is a law of nature; as such it belongs in the philosophical order of necessity. That Hector should die at an appointed time and under definite circumstances is an event in a particular human life. Behind necessity, there is a law; behind Fate, there is a will.

The same relation which obtains between

necessity and fate also obtains between the philosophical notion of cause and the Greek notion of the gods. A first cause, or principle, is a universally valid explanation for all that is, has ever been, or ever shall be. As an object of scientific or of philosophical knowledge, man is but one among the countless things that are possible objects of empirical observation and of rational explanation. When he looks at his own life as a scientist or as a philosopher, any man views its successive events, and he foresees his own death, as just so many particular effects of impersonal causes. But it so happens that every man is personally acquainted with a type of cause widely different from the scientific and philosophical ones. Man knows himself. Because he knows himself, man can say "I am." And because he knows other things besides himself, he can say of these things: "They are." A fact of tremendous importance indeed, since it is through human knowledge and, as far as we can see, through it alone that the world can achieve the awareness of its own existence. Hence, for the philosophers and the scientists of all times a first not inconsiderable difficulty: since man as a knowing being is part of the world, how to account for nature without ascribing to its first principle either knowledge or something which, because it virtually contains it, is actually superior to it?

From this same presence of knowledge in the world, a second difficulty arises, which is a still more considerable one. As a knowing being, man is able to distinguish between things, to become acquainted with their specific natures, and consequently to determine his own attitude toward things after his own knowledge of what they are. Now to be not determined by things but regulated by one's own knowledge of things is precisely what we call to be free. By introducing into the world a certain possibility of choice, knowledge brings about a curious sort of being which not only is, or exists, like all the rest, but which is, or exists, for itself; and for which alone all the rest appears as a set of actually existing things. Such a being—and I beg to remind you that its existence is an observable fact—cannot but be conscious of the exceptional situation it occupies in the universe. In a sense, it is but a part of the whole and, as such, completely submitted to the laws of the whole. In another sense, it is itself a whole, because it is an original center of spontaneous reactions and of free decisions. We call such a being man; we say that, since man directs his acts according to his knowledge, he has a will. As a cause, a human will is most unlike any other known sort of cause, for it is the only known one to be confronted by possible choices and to be an original power of self-determination. By far the hardest problem for philosophy and for science is to account for the existence of human wills in the world without ascribing to the first principle either a will or something which, because it virtually contains will, is actually superior to it.

To understand this is also to reach the deeply hidden source of Greek mythology, and therefore of Greek religion. The Greek gods are the crude but telling expression of this absolute conviction that since man is somebody, and not merely something, the ultimate explanation for what happens to him should rest with somebody, and not merely with something. As a stream of water running between muddy banks, Skamandros is but a river, that is, a thing; but as a Trojan river which boldly opposes the will of fleet-foot Achilles, it cannot be but a thing. Then does Skamandros appear in the semblance of a man, or rather of a superman, that is to say, of a god. Mythology is not a first step on the path to true philosophy. In fact, it is no philosophy at all. Mythology is a first step on the path to true religion; it is religious in its own right. Greek philosophy cannot have emerged from Greek mythology by any process of progressive rationalization,[20] because Greek philosophy was a rational attempt to understand the world as a world of things, whereas Greek mythology expressed the firm decision of man not to be left alone, the only person in a world of deaf and dumb things.

If this be true, we should not be surprised to see very great Greek philosophers at a loss how to identify their principles with their gods, or their gods with their principles. They needed them both. When Plato says of something that it truly is, or exists, he always means to say that its nature is both necessary and intelligible. Material and sensible things, for instance, cannot truly be said to be, for the simple reason that, ceaselessly changing

20. The theology of Hesiod is much more systematic than the loose theological elements scattered throughout the whole work of Homer. Hence some historians feel strongly inclined to consider it as marking a transitional stage on the road from primitive Greek mythology to early Greek philosophy. Their main argument is the rational tendency, so apparent in the *Theogony* of Hesiod, to reduce Greek mythology to some sort of systematic unity (see L. Robin, *La Pensée grecque* [Paris, 1923], p. 33, interpreted by R. K. Hack, *op. cit.*, p. 24). The fact itself is correct, but a rationally handled theology still remains a theology; a systematically organized mythology is a more rational theology than a loose one, but it is not an inch nearer to being a philosophy.

as they are, none of them ever remains the same during two successive instants. As soon as you know one of them, it vanishes, or else it alters its appearance, so that your knowledge either has completely lost its object, or no longer answers its object. How then could material things be intelligible? Man can know only that which is. Truly *to be* means to be immaterial, immutable, necessary, and intelligible. That is precisely what Plato calls Idea. The eternal and intelligible Ideas are reality itself. Not this and that particular man, but their unchangeable essence. The only thing that truly is, or exists, in a given individual, is not that accidental combination of characters which constitutes him as distinct from every other individual within the same species; it is rather his own sharing in the eternal essence of this species. Not Socrates as Socrates, or Callias as Callias, is truly a real being; in so far as they really are, Socrates and Callias are one and the same thing, namely Man-in-Himself, or the Idea of Man.

Such is Plato's view of reality when he sees it as an object of philosophical knowledge. Let us now ask ourselves what can deserve the title of divine in such a philosophy? If that which is the more real is also the more divine, the eternal Ideas should eminently deserve to be called divine. Now, among the Ideas there is one which dominates all the others, because they all share in its intelligibility. It is the Idea of Good. Just as among the gods in heaven the sun is the lord of all that shares in the essence of light, the Idea of Good dominates the intelligible world because all that is, in so far as it is, is good. Why then should we hesitate to conclude that in Plato's philosophy the Idea of Good is god?

I am far from disputing the logical validity of such a deduction. Plato should have made it. I even agree that we can hardly refrain from reading as a definition of his own god the famous lines of the *Republic* where Plato says of the Idea of Good that it is "the universal author of all things beautiful and right, parent of light and of the lord of light in the visible world, and the immediate source of reason and truth in the intellectual; and that this is the power upon which he who would act rationally either in public or private life must have his eye fixed."[21] Assuredly, nothing more closely resembles the definition of the Christian God than this definition of the Good.[22]

21. Plato, *Republic,* 517; quoted from *The Dialogues of Plato,* trans. B. Jowett, published with an Introduction by Prof. Raphael Demos (New York, 1937), I, 776.

22. A. J. Festugière, O.P., *op. cit.,* p. 191; by the same author, *Contemplation et vie contemplative selon Platon*

Yet, when all is said, the fact remains that Plato himself has never called the Good a god. To persuade his historians that since Plato himself does not say that the Good is a god we had better not make him say it would be a practically desperate undertaking. Even non-Christian interpreters of Plato have read Christian theology into his philosophy, after which they found it easy to demonstrate that Christian theology was but a corrupt edition of Plato's philosophy. It should be permitted, however, to suggest that if Plato has never said that the Idea of Good is a god, the reason for it might be that he never thought of it as of a god. And why, after all, should an Idea be considered as a god? An Idea is no person; it is not even a soul; at best it is an intelligible cause, much less a person than a thing.[23]

(Paris, J. Vrin, 1936). Cf. "Le Dieu de Platon," in A. Dies, *Autour de Platon* (Paris, G. Beauchesne, 1927), II, 523–574; and *La Religion de Platon,* pp. 575–602.

23. According to Festugière, the Idea of Good is "the most divine of all that which is divine," so that he who climbs the ladder of beings, from sensible things up to the highest of all Ideas, ultimately grasps the first Being; "he sees God" (*L'Idéal religieux des Grecs et l'Évangile,* p. 44; cf. p. 54). In the texts of *Republic,* 508a–509c, 517b–c, which Festugière quotes in support of his assertion, the sun and the stars are called gods, but not the Ideas. Even the Idea of Good is not called a god. The other references given by the same historian are *Republic,* 507b; *Phaedo,* 75d–e; *Parmenides,* 130b and ff.; *Philebus,* 15a. In not one of these texts have I been able to find

What makes it so hard for some modern scholars to reconcile themselves to this fact is that after so many centuries of Christian thought it has become exceedingly difficult for us to imagine a world where the gods are not the highest reality, while that which is the most supremely real in it is not a god. It is a fact, however, that in Plato's mind the gods were inferior to the Ideas. The Sun, for instance, was held by Plato as a god; and yet in his doctrine the Sun, who is a god, is a child of the Good, which is not a god. In order to understand Plato's own idea of a god, we must first imagine some individual living being, similar to those we know from sensible experience; but instead of imagining it as changeable,

the name of "god" attached by Plato to any Idea. In *Republic,* 508, it is said that the sun, whose soul is a god, is the child of the Good, but it is not said that the Good is a god. In *Phaedrus,* 247, Plato describes the "intangible essence, visible only to mind" (Jowett trans., I, 252), then Justice, Temperance, and Knowledge, as the heavenly objects of contemplation for "the divine Intelligence," but the Intelligence alone is here called divine; its objects are not called "gods." In *Phaedo,* 80, the soul is called "divine," in contradistinction to its body; and where Plato adds (Jowett trans., I, 465) that "the soul is in the very likeness of the divine, and immortal, and intellectual, and uniform, and indissoluble, and unchangeable," even if it had to be granted that he is here speaking of the Ideas, not of the other gods, Plato would have simply said that the Ideas are divine, not that they are gods. The identification of the Platonic Ideas with gods is still waiting for its historical justification.

contingent, and mortal, we must conceive it as intelligible, immutable, necessary, and eternal. This is a god for Plato. In short, a Platonic god is a living individual endowed with all the fundamental attributes of an Idea. This is the reason why a Platonic Idea can be more divine than a god, and yet not be a god. If we take man as a body quickened by a soul, man is mortal and corruptible; hence he is not a god. On the contrary, human souls are such living individual beings as are of intelligible nature and immortal in their own right; hence the human souls are gods. There are many gods higher than our own souls, but none of them is an Idea. There are the Olympians, whom Plato does not take too seriously, but nevertheless preserves after purifying them of their human weaknesses; after them come the gods of the state; then the gods below, without forgetting the demons or spirits, the heroes, "and after them . . . the private and ancestral gods who are worshipped as the law prescribes in the places which are sacred to them."[24] Clearly enough, the world of Plato is

24. Plato, *Republic,* 717, Jowett trans., II, 488. The historical problem, classical in the world of Platonic scholarship, whether or not the so-called "Creator" (or World-Maker) of the *Timaeus* (28 and ff.) is an Idea, should not even be asked. The "Creator" is a god working after the pattern of the eternal Ideas; he is a god-maker of other gods, such as the stars, the souls, and so on. Cf. *Laws,* X, 889, Jowett trans., II, 631.

no less full of gods than the world of Thales or that of Homer; and his gods are just as distinct from his philosophical principles as an order of persons is distinct from an order of things.

It is the presence of this world of divinities in Plato's dialogues which confers upon his doctrine its universally recognized religious character. Plato's religion is not to be looked for in the dialectical purification whereby the philosopher frees himself from his body and grows more and more comformable to the intelligible Ideas. When a philosopher thus reaches the intelligible world, he does not, strictly speaking, divinize his soul: his soul is a god in its own right. He does not even, strictly speaking, immortalize his soul: his soul is an indestructible life; it is immortal in its own right. A philosopher is a human soul which remembers its own divinity and behaves as becomes a god. The true religion of Plato consists in his feeling of adoration toward the innumerable gods to whom men pray and whom they invoke in their individual needs as well as in the needs of their cities. As a philosopher Plato writes his *Timaeus;* as a religious man, Plato invokes the gods and the goddesses of the world he is about to describe, before beginning to descibe it.[25] Just like any

25. Plato, *Timaeus,* 27, Jowett trans., II, 12.

other man, Plato needs to feel himself surrounded with personal powers which take care of his own life and of his own destiny. Typically enough, the main attribute of a Platonic god is to be a providence to man.[26] Owing to the friendly presence of his divinities, Plato does not feel himself alone in a chaotic desert of inanimate things. "All things are full of gods," Plato expressly repeats after Thales, and he can never think too highly of his divine protectors. "You have a low opinion of mankind, Stranger," Megillus says in the VII Book of *Laws;* and the Athenian's answer is: "Nay, Megillus, be not amazed, but forgive me:—I was comparing them with the gods."[27]

This description of Plato's religious attitude not only clears up some aspects of his doctrine but also enables us to grasp, at its point of emergence, the philosophical notion of god. Plato, who seems to have invented the Ideas as a philosophical principle of explanation, did not invent the gods. They appear in his doctrine as a legacy of Greek mythology, and this is why they play so large a part in

26. Plato, *Laws,* X, 888, Jowett trans., II, 630. Cf. *ibid.,* X, 899–907, II, 641–649. The conclusion of this text is "that the Gods exist, and that they take care of men, and that they can never be persuaded to do injustice." *Laws,* X, 907, II, 649.

27. *Ibid.,* VII, 804, Jowett trans., II, 559.

Plato's myths. Time and again the philosopher reminds us that the belief of men in the existence of the gods is a very ancient and therefore a venerable one. This avowedly inherited belief however is susceptible of some rational justification. And the way Plato justifies it is highly suggestive. Every time we see a living thing and self-moving thing, quickened from within by a spontaneous power of operation, we can be sure that such a thing has a soul; and since every soul is a god, each living thing is inhabited by a god. Such are, for instance, the sun and the other stars, whose perpetual revolutions witness to the presence in them of some divinity. In other words, the soul is to Plato the very pattern after which men have formed their notion of god. Were it not for human souls, how could you account for the spontaneous motion of human bodies? But then, Plato adds, how are you to account for the spontaneous motion of the stars, unless you ascribe to each of them some sort of soul? If you do, you must acknowledge at the same time that each and every star is inhabited by a god.[28]

28. *Ibid.,* X, 899, II, 641. Cf. XII, 966–967, II, 700–702. For a criticism of the fabulous mythology of Homer and Hesiod, see *Republic,* II, 377–378, Jowett trans., I, 641–642.

In his own objective and matter of fact manner, Aristotle has drawn from Plato's demonstration the lesson it teaches concerning the origin of our philosophical notion of god. Men, Aristotle says, have derived it from two sources: their own souls and the motion of the stars.[29] And if we remember the gods of Homer, it is at once apparent that Aristotle was right.

What makes Aristotle's metaphysics an epoch-making event in the history of natural theology is that in it the long delayed conjunction of the first philosophical principle with the notion of god became at last an accomplished fact. The prime mover of the Aristotelian universe is also its supreme god. And thus to become a god was an appreciable gain for the first philosophical principle and supreme cause of the world, but thus to become just so many philosophical principles was to prove a most perilous adventure for the whole family of the Greek gods. That the old Olympians had then to step out of the picture was a gain rather than a loss, not only to philoso-

29. Aristotle, "fragment 12," in *Aristotelis Opera* (Berlin, 1870), V, 1475–1476. In dreams and in divination, the soul seems to behave as if it were a god; as to the stars, their orderly motion suggests that there are causes of their motion and of their order. Each one of these causes is a god.

phy, but even to religion. The real danger, for what was still going to be left of the gods, was that of losing their very divinity.

The world of Aristotle is there, as something that has always been and always will be. It is an eternally necessary and a necessarily eternal world. The problem for us is therefore not to know how it has come into being but to understand what happens in it and consequently what it is. At the summit of the Aristotelian universe is not an Idea but a self-subsisting and eternal Act of thinking. Let us call it Thought: a divine self-thinking Thought. Below it are the concentric heavenly spheres, each of which is eternally moved by a distinct Intelligence, which itself is a distinct god. From the eternal motion of these spheres the generation and corruption, that is, the birth and death, of all earthly things are eternally caused. Obviously, in such a doctrine, the theological interpretation of the world is one with its philosophical and scientific explanation.[30] The only question is: Can we still have a religion? The pure Act of the self-thinking Thought eternally thinks of itself, but never of us. The supreme god of Aristotle has not made this world of ours; he

30. On the self-thinking Thought of Aristotle, see his *Metaphysics,* Bk. XI, chaps. vii and ix.

does not even know it as distinct from himself, nor, consequently, can he take care of any one of the beings or things that are in it. It is true each human individual is endowed with a soul of his own, but this soul is no longer an immortal god like the Platonic soul; a physical form of a material and perishable body, the soul of man is doomed to perish with it. Perhaps we ought to love the god of Aristotle, but what would be the use, since this god himself does not love us? From time to time a few wise men succeed in sharing for a fleeting moment in the eternal beatitude of the divine contemplation. But even when philosophers succeed in descrying from afar the highest truth, their beatitude is a short-lived one, and philosophers are scarce. Truly wise men do not play at being gods; they rather aim to achieve the practical wisdom of moral and political life. God is in his heaven; it is up to men to take care of the world. With Aristotle, the Greeks had gained an indisputably rational theology, but they had lost their religion.

Once freed by the philosophers from the care of earthly things, the Greek gods seem to have renounced, once and for all, their former interest in man and his destiny. The popular gods of Greek mythology have never ceased to perform their religious functions, but the rationalized gods of the philosophers no longer had any religious function to perform. In the doctrine of Epicurus, for instance, the gods are so many eternally subsisting material beings, whose perfect blessedness entails that they should never worry about anything else, particularly about men.[31] As to the great Stoics, it is impossible to open their works without meeting there, in practically every chapter, the name of god. But what is their god, if not fire, the material element out of which this universe is made? Owing to it, the world is one; an all-pervading harmony, or sympathy, links together its parts, and each of us is in it, as one of its many parts: "For there is both one Universe, made up of all things, and one God immanent in all things, and one Substance, and one Law, one Reason common to all intelligent creatures, and one Truth." Since we find ourselves in the world as in the City of Zeus, to love it is for us by far the wisest course to follow.[32] Whether we like it or not, however, we shall have to yield

31. On the survival of Aristotelian elements in the Epicurean notion of the gods, see the excellent remarks of A. J. Festugière, O.P., *op. cit.*, p. 63.

32. *The Communings with Himself of Marcus Aurelius*, text and trans. by C. R. Haines (London, 1916), Loeb Classical Library. Cf. Bk. VII, 9, p. 169 and Bk. IV, 23, p. 81.

to the necessity of its laws: "The World-Cause is a torrent," Marcus Aurelius says, "it sweeps everything along."[33] And again: "The Nature of the Whole felt impelled to the creation of a Universe; but now either all that comes into being does so by a natural sequence, or even the most paramount things, toward which the ruling Reason of the Universe feels an impulse of its own, are devoid of intelligence. Recollect this and thou wilt face many an ill with more serenity."[34]

It has been said of Marcus Aurelius that he has not had the god he deserved. It might still more truly be said that Marcus Aurelius has had no god at all. His piety toward god is but a wise resignation to what he knows to be inevitable. "A little while and thou wilt have forgotten everything, a little while and everything will have forgotten thee."[35] These words of the great Stoic also are the last words of Greek wisdom, and they clearly mark the fail-

33. *Ibid.*, Bk. IX, 29, pp. 247–248.

34. *Ibid.*, Bk. VII, 75, p. 197.

35. *Ibid.*, Bk. VII, 22, p. 173. Even in Marcus Aurelius, the gods are still present as friendly powers who take care of men and do their best to protect them from evil (see, for instance, Bk. II, 11, pp. 32–35); but the gods of Marcus Aurelius play an infinitesimal part in his doctrine; even their good will does not inspire him with any more cheerful feeling than an almost desperate resignation.

ure of the Greeks to build up an all-comprehensive philosophical explanation of the world without at the same time losing their religion. In the light of what precedes, the reason for their failure is at hand. A Greek philosophical interpretation of the world is an explanation of what natures are, by what a certain nature is; in other words, the Greeks have consistently tried to explain all things by means of one or several principles themselves considered as things. Now, men can be preached into worshiping any living being, from a wholly imaginary one like Zeus to a wholly ridiculous one like the Golden Calf. Provided only it be somebody or something which they can mistake for somebody, they may eventually worship it. What men cannot possibly bring themselves to do is to worship a thing. When Greek philosophy came to an end, what was sorely needed for progress in natural theology was progress in metaphysics. Such philosophical progress was to be made as early as the fourth century A.D.; but, curiously enough, metaphysics was to make it under the influence of religion.

II

GOD AND CHRISTIAN PHILOSOPHY

WHILE the Greek philosophers were wondering what place to assign to their gods in a philosophically intelligible world, the Jews had already found the God who was to provide philosophy with an answer to its own question. Not a God imagined by poets or discovered by any thinker as an ultimate answer to his metaphysical problems, but one who had revealed Himself to the Jews, told them His name, and explained to them His nature, in so far at least as His nature can be understood by men.

The first character of the Jewish God was his unicity: "Hear, O Israel: the Lord our God is one Lord."[1] Impossible to achieve a more far-reaching revolution in fewer words or in a simpler way. When Moses made this statement, he was not formulating any metaphysical principle to be later supported by rational justification. Moses was simply speaking as an inspired prophet and defining for the benefit of the Jews what was henceforth to be the sole object of their worship. Yet, es-

1. Deuteronomy 6.4.

sentially religious as it was, this statement contained the seed of a momentous philosophical revolution, in this sense at least, that should any philosopher, speculating at any time about the first principle and cause of the world, hold the Jewish God to be the true God, he would be necessarily driven to identify his supreme philosophical cause with God. In other words, whereas the difficulty was, for a Greek philosopher, to fit a plurality of gods into a reality which he conceived as one, any follower of the Jewish God would know at once that, whatever the nature of reality itself may be said to be, its religious principle must of necessity coincide with its philosophical principle. Each of them being one, they are bound to be the same and to provide men with one and the same explanation of the world.

When the existence of this one true God was proclaimed by Moses to the Jews, they never thought for a moment that their Lord could be some thing. Obviously, their Lord was somebody. Besides, since he was the God of the Jews, they already knew Him; and they knew Him as the Lord God of their fathers, the God of Abraham, the God of Isaac, and the God of Jacob. Time and again, their God had proved to them that He was taking care of His people; their relations with

Him had always been personal relations, that is, relations between persons and another person; the only thing they still wanted to know about Him was what to call Him. As a matter of fact, Moses himself did not know the name of the one God; but he knew that the Jews would ask him for it; and instead of engaging upon deep metaphysical meditations to discover the true name of God, he took a typically religious short cut. Moses simply asked God about His name, saying to Him: "Lo, I shall go to the children of Israel, and say to them: The God of your fathers hath sent me to you. If they should say to me: What is His name? What shall I say to them? God said to Moses: I AM WHO AM. He said: Thus shalt thou say to the children of Israel: HE WHO IS, hath sent me to you."[2] Hence the universally known name of the Jewish God—Yahweh, for Yahweh means "He who is."

Here again historians of philosophy find themselves confronted with this to them always unpalatable fact: a nonphilosophical statement which has since become an epoch-making statement in the history of philosophy. The Jewish genius was not a philosophical genius; it was a religious one. Just as the Greeks are our masters in philosophy, the

2. Exodus 3.13–14.

Jews are our masters in religion. So long as the Jews kept their own religious revelation to themselves, nothing happened to philosophy. But owing to the preaching of the Gospel the God of the Jews ceased to be the private God of an elect race and became the universal God of all men. Any Christian convert who was at all familiar with Greek philosophy was then bound to realize the metaphysical import of his new religious belief. His philosophical first principle had to be one with his religious first principle, and since the name of his God was "I am," any Christian philosopher had to posit "I am" as his first principle and supreme cause of all things, even in philosophy. To use our own modern terminology, let us say that a Christian's philosophy is "existential" in its own right.

This point was of such importance that even the earliest Christian thinkers did not fail to see it. When the first educated Greeks became converts to Christianity, the Olympian gods of Homer had already been discredited as mere mythical imaginings through the repeated criticism of the philosophers. But those very philosophers had no less completely discredited themselves by giving to the world the spectacle of their endless contradictions. Even those who were the greatest among them, taken at their very best, had never succeeded in correctly stating what they at least should have held to be the supreme cause of all things. Plato, for instance, had clearly seen that the ultimate philosophical explanation for all that which is should ultimately rest, not within those elements of reality that are always being generated and therefore never really are, but with something which, because it has no generation, truly is, or exists. Now, as has been pointed out by the unknown author of the *Hortatory Address to the Greeks* as early as the third century A.D. what Plato had said was almost exactly what the Christians themselves were saying, "saving only the difference of the article. For Moses said: *He who is*, and Plato: *That which is*." And it is quite true that "either of the expressions seems to apply to the existence of God."[3] If God is "He who is," he also is "that which is," because to be somebody is also to be something. Yet the converse is not true, for to be somebody is much more than to be something.

We are here at the dividing line between Greek thought and Christian thought, that is

3. *Hortatory Address to the Greeks*, chap. xxii, published among the works of Justin Martyr, in *The Ante-Nicene Fathers* (Buffalo, 1885), I, 272. Cf. E. Gilson, *L'Esprit de la philosophie médiévale* (Paris, J. Vrin, 1932), I, 227, n. 7.

to say, between Greek philosophy and Christian philosophy. Taken in itself, Christianity was not a philosophy. It was the essentially religious doctrine of the salvation of men through Christ. Christian philosophy arose at the juncture of Greek philosophy and of the Jewish-Christian religious revelation, Greek philosophy providing the technique for a rational explanation of the world, and the Jewish-Christian revelation providing religious beliefs of incalculable philosophical import. What is perhaps the key to the whole history of Christian philosophy and, in so far as modern philosophy bears the mark of Christian thought, to the history of modern philosophy itself, is precisely the fact that, from the second century A.D. on, men have had to use a Greek philosophical technique in order to express ideas that had never entered the head of any Greek philosopher.

This was by no means an easy task. The Greeks had never gone further than the natural theology of Plato and of Aristotle, not on account of intellectual weakness on their part, but, on the contrary, because both Plato and Aristotle had pushed their investigations almost as far as human reason alone can take us. By positing, as the supreme cause of all that which is, somebody who is, and of whom the very best that can be said is that "He is," Christian revelation was establishing existence as the deepest layer of reality as well as the supreme attribute of the divinity. Hence, in so far as the world itself was concerned, the entirely new philosophical problem of its very existence, and the still deeper one whose formula runs thus: What is it to exist? As Professor J. B. Muller-Thym aptly remarks, where a Greek simply asks: What is nature? a Christian rather asks: What is being?[4]

The first epoch-making contact between Greek philosophical speculation and Christian religious belief took place when, already a convert to Christianity, the young Augustine began to read the works of some Neo-Platonists, particularly the *Enneads* of Plotinos.[5]

4. J. B. Muller-Thym, *On the University of Being in Meister Eckhart of Hochheim* (New York, Sheed and Ward, 1939), p. 2.

5. For a good introduction to the many interpretations of this historical fact, see Charles Boyer, S.J., *La Formation de saint Augustin* (Paris, Beauchesne, 1920). An exactly opposite view is maintained by P. Alfaric, *L'Évolution intellectuelle de saint Augustin* (Paris, Nourry, 1918). The very nature of the problem entails psychological hypotheses which cannot be either historically demonstrated or historically refuted. I feel personally convinced that the views of C. Boyer on the question are fundamentally sound, but nobody should subscribe to them before carefully weighing the arguments set forward by Alfaric in support of his own interpretation.

Augustine found there, not the pure philosophy of Plato, but an original synthesis of Plato, Aristotle, and the Stoics. Moreover, even where he borrowed from Plato, Plotinos had identified the Idea of Good, as described in the *Republic*, with that other puzzling principle, the One, which makes its late appearance in Plato's *Parmenides*. The very conclusion of this dialogue seems to have provided Plotinos with the keystone of his own metaphysical system: "Then were we to say in a word: if the one is not, nothing is, should we be right?—Most assuredly." And indeed, if the One is that without which nothing else could be, the existence of the whole world must of necessity depend upon some eternally subsisting Unity.

Let us then imagine, with Plotinos, a first principle whom we will call the One. Strictly speaking, he is unnamable because he cannot be described. Any attempt at expressing him must of necessity result in a judgment, and since a judgment is made up of several terms, we cannot say what the One is without turning his unity into some sort of multiplicity, that is, without destroying it. Let us say then that he is the One, not as a number that can enter the composition of other numbers, nor as a synthesis of other numbers, but as the self-subsisting unity whence all multiplicity follows without affecting in the least its absolute simplicity. From the fecundity of the One a second principle is born, inferior to the first, yet eternally subsisting like the One and, after him, the cause of all that comes after him. His name is the Intellect. Unlike the One, the Intellect is the self-subsisting knowledge of all that is intelligible. Since he himself is both the knowing subject and the known object, he is as near being the One as it is possible to be; yet since he is affected by the duality of subject and object inherent in all knowledge, he is not the One; consequently he is inferior to him.

Among the attributes which belong to the Intellect, two are of particular importance for a correct understanding of our historical problem. Conceived as an eternally subsisting cognition of all that which is intelligible, the Intellect of Plotinos is, by definition, the locus of all the Ideas. They are in him as a multiple intelligible unity; they are eternally sharing in the fecundity which he himself owes to the fecundity of the One; in short, the Intellect is big with all that multiplicity of individual and distinct beings which eternally flow from him. In this sense, he is a god and the father of all the other gods.

A second characteristic of the Intellect, much harder to grasp than the preceding one, is perhaps still more important. When can we say of anything: It is? As soon as, by an act of understanding, we apprehend it as distinct from something else. In other words, so long as nothing is actually understood, nothing is; which amounts to saying that being first appears in, by, and with this Intellect, who is the second principle in Plotinos' philosophy. These are the two supreme causes of the Plotinian universe: at the top, the One of Plato's *Parmenides;* immediately below him, and born of him, the self-thinking Thought of Aristotle, whom Plotinos calls the Nous, or Intellect, and whom he conceives as the locus of Plato's Ideas. Such also were the main data of the problem which Augustine boldly undertook to solve: how to express the God of Christianity in terms borrowed from the philosophy of Plotinos?

If we look at this problem as historians, and view it through fifteen centuries of history, our first impulse is to declare that such a problem was not susceptible of a satisfactory solution. Perhaps it was not. But we should remember that the creations of the human mind do not obey the analytical laws which preside over their historical explanations. What appears to us as a problem fraught with tremendous difficulties was never perceived by Augustine as a problem; the only thing he was ever aware of was its solution.

Generations after generations of historians have pondered over this extraordinary and, in a way, inexplicable phenomenon. Here is a young convert to Christianity who, for the first time in his life, reads the *Enneads* of Plotinos, and what he sees there at once is the Christian God himself, with all his essential attributes. Who is the One, if not God the Father, the first person of the Christian Trinity? And who is the Nous, or Intellect, if not the second person of the Christian Trinity, that is, the Word, exactly as he appears at the beginning of the Gospel of Saint John? "And therein I read, not indeed in the same words, but to the selfsame effect, enforced by many and divers reasons, that: In the beginning was the Word, and the Word with with God, and the Word was God. All things were made by Him; and without Him was not any thing made that was made."[6] In short, as soon as Augustine read the *Enneads*, he found there

6. Saint Augustine, *Confessions,* Bk. VII, chap. ix, n. 13, trans. by the Rev. Marcus Dods, in "The Works of Aurelius Augustine" (Edinburgh, 1876), XIV, 152–153.

the three essentially Christian notions of God the Father, of God the Word, and of the creation.

That Augustine found them there is an incontrovertible fact. That they were not there is a hardly more controvertible fact. To go at once to the fundamental reason why they could not possibly be there, let us say that the world of Plotinos and the world of Christianity are strictly incomparable; no single point in the one can be matched with any single point in the other one, for the fundamental reason that their metaphysical structure is essentially different. Plotinos was living in the third century A.D.; yet his philosophical thought remained wholly foreign to Christianity. His world is a Greek philosophical world, made up of natures whose operations are strictly determined by their essences. Even the One of Plotinos, whom we can hardly refrain from designating as a He, exists and operates after the manner of an It. If we compare him to the rest, the One, or Good, is absolutely free, because all the rest depends upon him for its existence, whereas he himself, being the first principle, does not depend upon anything else. Taken in himself, on the contrary, the One is strictly determined by his own nature; not only the One is what he has to be, but he acts as he has to act on account of what he necessarily is. Hence the typically Greek aspect of the Plotinian universe as a natural, eternal, and necessary generation of all things by the One. Everything eternally flows from him as a radiation which he himself does not even know, because he is above thought, above being, above the duality of being and thought. In Plotinos' own words: "As to the unbegotten principle, who has nothing above him, who is eternally what he is, what reason might he have to think?"[7]

To Plotinos' question, let our answer be: No reason whatsoever; but let us immediately add that this alone is a sufficient reason why the god of Plotinos cannot possibly be the Christian God nor the world of Plotinos a Christian world. The Plotinian universe is typically Greek in this, that in it God is neither the supreme reality nor the ultimate principle of intelligibility. Hence this metaphysically momentous consequence, that the dividing line between the first cause and all the rest does not coincide in a philosophy of the One and in a philosophy of being. Since nothing can beget itself, what the One begets

7. Plotinos, *Enneads,* VI, 7, 37, in "Complete Works," trans. by Kenneth Sylvan Guthrie (Alpine, N. J., Platonist Press), III, 762.

has to be other than the One; consequently, it must of necessity be multiple. This applies even to the Intellect, who is the highest Plotinian god. The Plotinian dividing line thus cuts off the One, who is the only unbegotten principle, from all the begotten multiplicity, that is to say, from all the rest. In all the rest are to be found the Intellect, who is the first god, followed by the supreme Soul, who is the second god, then all the other gods including the human souls. In other words, while there is a radical difference of nature between the One, or Good, and all that which, because it is not the One, is multiple, there are but differences of degrees between all that which is not the One, and yet is, or exists. We ourselves belong in the same metaphysical class as the Intellect and the supreme Soul; we are gods just as they are, begotten from the One just as they are, and inferior to them, in proportion to our respective degrees of multiplicity, as they themselves are inferior to the One.

Not so in a Christian metaphysics of being, where the supreme principle is a God whose true name is "He who is." A pure Act of existing, taken as such and without any limitation, necessarily is all that which it is possible to be. We cannot even say that such a God has knowledge, or love, or anything else; he is it in his own right, for the very reason that, were he not everything and anything that it is possible to be, he could be called "He who is" but with some added qualification. If, as is part of Christian faith, such a God begets in virtue of his infinite fecundity, he must beget somebody else, that is another person, but not something else, that is another God. Otherwise, there would be two absolute acts of existing, each of which would include the totality of being, which is absurd. If, on the other hand, such a God actually is, or exists, his self-sufficiency is so perfect that there can be no necessity for anything else to exist. Nothing can be added to him; nothing can be subtracted from him; and since nothing can share in his being without at once being himself; "He who is" can eternally enjoy the fullness of his own perfection, of his own beatitude, without needing to grant existence to anybody else, or to anything whatsoever.

Yet it is a fact that there is something which is not God. Men, for instance, are not such an eternal act of absolute existence. There are therefore some beings that are radically different from God at least in this that, unlike him, they might not have existed, and still may, at a certain time, cease to exist. Thus to be, or exist, is not at all to be, or exist, as God himself is, or exists. It is therefore not to be an inferior sort of god; rather, it is not to be a god at all. The only possible explanation for the presence of such finite and contingent beings is that they have been freely given existence by "Him who is," and not as parcels of his own existence, which, because it is absolute and total, is also unique, but as finite and partial imitations of what He himself eternally is in his own right. This act whereby "He who is" causes to exist something that, of itself, is not, is what is called, in Christian philosophy, "creation." Whence there follows, that whereas all that which the Christian God begets must of necessity share in the oneness of God, all that which does not share in his oneness must of necessity be not begotten but created.

Such is, in fact, the Christian world of Saint Augustine. On the one side, God, one in the Trinity of a single, self-existing substance; on the other side, all that which, because it has but a received existence, is not God. Unlike the Plotinian dividing line which we have seen running between the One and all that is begotten by the One, the Christian dividing line runs between God, including his own begotten Word, and all that is created by God. As one among God's creatures, man finds himself therein excluded from the order of the divine. Between "Him who is" and ourselves, there is the infinite metaphysical chasm which separates the complete self-sufficiency of His own existence from the intrinsic lack of necessity of our own existence. Nothing can bridge such a chasm, save a free act of the divine will only. This is why, from the time of Saint Augustine up to our own days, human reason has been up against the tremendously difficult task of reaching a transcendent God whose pure act of existing is radically distinct from our own borrowed existence. How can man, who out of himself is not, living in a world of things which out of themselves are not, reach, by means of reason alone, "Him who is"? Such is, to a Christian, the fundamental problem of natural theology.

In his effort to solve this problem, Augustine had nothing to help him but the philosophical technique of Plato in the revised edition of Plotinos. Here again, the philosophical eagerness of the Christian convert took him beyond the data of the problem straight to its solution. Interpreting Plato's doctrine of reminiscence, Plotinos had described dialectics as an effort of the human soul to rid itself of all material images so as to contemplate the intelligible Ideas in the light of the first Intellect, who is the supreme god. Was not this exactly what Saint John himself had, if not philosophically established, at least clearly suggested in the first chapter of his gospel? When Plotinos and Saint John thus met in the mind of Augustine, their combination was instantaneous. Reading the gospel into Plotinos' *Enneads*, he found there that the soul of man, though it "bears witness of the light," yet itself "is not that light; but the Word of God, being God, is that true light that lighteth every man that cometh into the world."[8] Why should not men use this constant presence of the divine light in their souls as an always open way to the Christian God?

This is precisely what Augustine did, or, at least, what he tried to do, for the task proved to be a much more difficult one than he himself had imagined. In inheriting the philosophical world of Plato, Augustine had fallen heir to Plato's man. Now, man, as Plato conceived him, was not the substantial unity of body and soul; he was essentially a soul. Instead of saying that man *has* a soul, we should therefore say that man *is* a particular soul, that is to say, an intelligent, intelligible, and eternally

8. Saint John, 1. 7–9. Cf. Saint Augustine, *op. cit.*, Bk. VII, chap. ix, n. 13, English trans., p. 154. The text of Saint John directly applies to the problem of human salvation through Christ.

living substance, which, though it now happens to be conjoined to a body, has always existed before it and is ultimately destined to outlive it. In Plato's own words, man is "a soul using a body,"[9] but he is no more his body than a worker is the tools he uses or than any one of us is his own garments.

By accepting this definition of man, Augustine was putting himself in an exceedingly awkward philosophical position. In Plato's doctrine, and still more clearly in that of Plotinos, to be a purely intelligible, living, and immortal substance was exactly to be a god. Human souls then are just so many gods. When a man philosophizes and, discarding his body, focuses his mind upon intelligible truth, he simply behaves like a god who remembers to be a god. Rightly to philosophize then is nothing else, for each and every one of us, than to behave as becomes the god which each and every one of us actually is. True, we all are but individual Intelligences radiated by the supreme Intellect, and therefore by the One. For this very reason, just as we are by and in the One, we also know, and contem-

9. Plato, *Alcibiades,* 129e–130c. Saint Augustine, *De Moribus ecclesiae,* Bk. I, chap. xxvii, p. 52; *Patrologia Latina,* Vol. XXXII, col. 1332. Cf. É. Gilson, *Introduction à l'étude de saint Augustin* (Paris, J. Vrin, 1929), p. 55.

plate, by and in the light of the supreme Intellect who eternally emanates from the One. Yet, when all is said and done, we nevertheless are so many gods, lesser gods as we may be, patiently working our way back into the company of our fellow gods. Dialectics, as Plato and Plotinos understood it, was but the method which enables man to achieve a sort of philosophical salvation, by progressively raising him to the full awareness of his own divinity. A god may eventually forget himself but he cannot possibly stand in need of being saved.[10]

This is the fundamental reason why Saint Augustine has found it so hard to reach the Christian God by means of methods borrowed from Plato and Plotinos. To him, as to them, all that was immaterial, intelligible, and true was divine in its own right; but, whereas, in Plato's philosophy, man was naturally entitled to the possession of truth as a divinity is entitled to the possession of things divine, he could no longer appear as entitled to it in a Christian philosophy where, metaphysically

10. On this problem, see the extremely important analyses of Marcel de Corte, *Aristôte et Plotin* (Paris, Desclée de Brouwer, 1935), chap. iii, "La Purification plotinienne," pp. 177–227, and chap. vi, "La Dialectique de Plotin," pp. 229–290. These two essays are probably the deepest existing introductions to the method and spirit of the doctrine of Plotinos.

speaking,[11] man in no way belongs in the divine order. Hence this important consequence, that man was bound to appear to Augustine as a creature endowed with something that was divine in its own right. If truth is divine, and if man is not a god, man should not be possessed of truth. In fact, however, man is; consequently, the only conceivable way for Augustine to account for the paradoxical presence of intelligible truth, which is divine, in man, who is not a god, was to consider man

11. I beg to stress the words "metaphysically speaking," in order to make clear the radical difference there is between the order of metaphysics and the order of religion. As a Christian, any man can be "deified" through grace, because grace is a sharing in the life of God. Thus understood, grace is supernatural in its own right. So also is the whole sacramental order, as clearly appears from the well-known prayer of the Ordinary of the Mass, which I beg to quote in full because of its perfect clarity: "O God, who in creating human nature hast wonderfully dignified it, and still more wonderfully reformed it; grant by the mystery of this Water and Wine, *we may be made partakers of His divine nature,* who vouchsafed to become partaker of our human nature, namely, Jesus Christ, our Lord, Thy Son, who with Thee, livest and reignest, in the unity of the Holy Ghost, God, world without end. Amen." The man of Plato stood in no need of being made partaker of the divinity, because he himself was a god; hence, for Augustine, the necessity of stripping the man of Plato of what made him a god, namely, his natural aptness to know truth. We will find Thomas Aquinas confronted with the contrary difficulty, namely, that of turning the eminently natural man of Aristotle into a being susceptible of deification.

as knowing in the permanent light of a supremely intelligible and self-subsisting truth, that is, in the light of God.

Time and again, under a variety of different forms, Augustine has attempted the same demonstration of the existence of God as the only conceivable cause of the presence of truth in the human mind. His God is the intelligible sun whose light shines upon human reason and enables it to know truth; he is the inner master who teaches man from within; his eternal and unchangeable ideas are the supreme rules whose influence submits our reason to the necessity of divine truth. As demonstrations, the arguments of Saint Augustine are very effective. Granting that truth is superhuman and divine in its own right, the bare fact that man knows truth conclusively proves the existence of God. But why should we grant Augustine that truth is a more than human object of knowledge? The only reason why he himself thought so was a merely accidental one. Augustine's implicit reasoning seems to have run as follows: Plato and Plotinos consider man as a god because man is possessed of truth; now man is emphatically not a god; hence man cannot possibly be possessed of truth. Taken in itself, such an argument is perfectly correct; it would even be a perfectly conclusive one if it were true to say that truth is too good a thing to be considered as naturally attainable by man.

What happened to Saint Augustine is only too clear. An unsurpassed exponent of Christian wisdom, he never had the philosophy of his theology. The God of Augustine is the true Christian God, of whose pure Act of existing nothing better can be said than: He is; but when Augustine undertakes to describe existence in philosophical terms, he at once falls back upon the Greek identification of being with the notions of immateriality, intelligibility, immutability, and unity. Every such thing is divine; since truth is such, truth is divine. Immaterial, intelligible, and immutable, truth belongs in the order of that which truly is, or exists. Consequently, it belongs to God. Similarly the God of Augustine is the true creator of all things; but when it comes to defining creation, Augustine naturally understands it in accordance with his own notion of being. To create is to give being, and since to be is to be both intelligible and one, Augustine understands creation as the divine gift of that sort of existence which consists in rhythm, numbers, forms, beauty, order, and unity.[12] Like all Christians, but unlike the Greeks, Augustine has a quite clear notion of what it is to create something "out of nothing." It is to make it to be. What still remains Greek in Augustine's thought is his very notion of what it is to be. His ontology, or science of being, is an "essential" rather than an "existential" one. In other words, it exhibits a marked tendency to reduce the existence of a thing to its essence, and to answer the question: What is it for a thing to be? by saying: It is to be that which it is.

A most sensible answer indeed, but perhaps not the deepest conceivable one in philosophy, and certainly not a perfectly suitable one for a Christian philosopher speculating on a world created by the Christian God. For reasons which I will later try to make clear, it was

12. On the metaphysical constituents of concrete existence, see Emmanuel Chapman, *Saint Augustine's Philosophy of Beauty* (New York, Sheed and Ward, 1939), chap. ii, pp. 13–44. The Platonic character of the Augustinian notion of creation has been stressed, and perhaps slightly overstressed, by A. Gardeil, *La Structure mystique de l'âme* (Paris, Gabalda, 1929), Appendix II, vol. II, 319–320. After rereading my own criticism of A. Gardeil's interpretation (in *Introduction à l'étude de saint Augustin,* p. 258, n. 8), I have reached the conclusion that what Gardeil had in mind when he wrote these pages was fundamentally true; yet I myself was not altogether wrong. Augustine had a clear idea of what it is to create, but he never reached a wholly existential notion of being.

not easy to go beyond Saint Augustine, because the limit he had reached was the limit of Greek ontology itself, and therefore just about the very limit which the human mind can reach in matters of metaphysics. When, nine centuries after the death of Saint Augustine, a new and decisive progress in natural theology was made, its occasional cause was the discovery of another Greek metaphysical universe by another Christian theologian. This time the metaphysical universe was that of Aristotle, and the name of the theologian was Thomas Aquinas.

"The religious side of Plato's thought," Gilbert Murray rightly says, "was not revealed in its full power till the time of Plotinos in the third century A.D.: that of Aristotle, one might say without undue paradox, not till its exposition by Aquinas in the thirteenth."[13] Let us add only this, that the "explanation" of Aristotle by Thomas Aquinas might perhaps be more justly called its metamorphosis in the light of Christian revelation. The self-thinking Thought of Aristotle has certainly become an essential element of the natural theology of Saint Thomas Aquinas, but not without first undergoing the meta-

13. Gilbert Murray, *Five Stages of Greek Religion* (New York, Columbia University Press, 1925), p. 17.

physical transformation that turned him into the *Qui est*, or "He who is" of the Old Testament.[14]

Why, Saint Thomas asks, do we say that *Qui est* is the most proper name among all those that can be given to God? And his answer is because it signifies "to be": *ipsum esse*. But what is it to be? In answering this most difficult of all metaphysical questions, we must carefully distinguish between the meaning of two words which are both different and yet intimately related: *ens*, or "being," and *esse*, or "to be." To the question: What is being? the correct answer is: Being is that which is, or exists. If, for instance, we ask this same question with regard to God, the correct answer would be: The being of God is an infinite and boundless ocean of substance.[15] But *esse*, or "to be," is something else and much harder to grasp because it lies more deeply hidden in the metaphysical structure of reality. The word "being," as a noun, designates some substance; the word "to be"—or *esse*—is a verb,

14. Saint Thomas Aquinas, *Summa theologica,* Pars I, qu. 13, art. 11, *Sed contra.* On the Thomistic identification of God with Being, see É. Gilson, *The Spirit of Mediaeval Philosophy* (New York, Scribners, 1936), chap. iii, pp. 42–63.

15. This formula is quoted from John Damascene by Saint Thomas Aquinas, *op. cit.,* Pars I, qu. 13, art. 11, *Resp.*

because it designates an act. To understand this is also to reach, beyond the level of essence, the deeper level of existence. For it is quite true to say that all that which is a substance must of necessity have also both an essence and an existence. In point of fact, such is the natural order followed by our rational knowledge: we first conceive certain beings, then we define their essences, and last we affirm their existences by means of a judgment. But the metaphysical order of reality is just the reverse of the order of human knowledge: what first comes into it is a certain act of existing which, because it is *this* particular act of existing, circumscribes at once a certain essence and causes a certain substance to come into being. In this deeper sense, "to be" is the primitive and fundamental act by virtue of which a certain being actually is, or exists. In Saint Thomas' own words: *dicitur esse ipse actus essentiae*[16]—"to be" is the very act whereby an essence is.

A world where "to be" is the act par excel-

16. Saint Thomas Aquinas, in I. *Sent.*, dist. 33, qu. 1, art. 1, ad 1^{m}. Cf. *Quaestiones disputatae: De Potentia,* qu. VII, art. 2, ad 9. This existential notion of being is discussed in É. Gilson, *Réalisme thomiste et critique de la connaissance* (Paris, J. Vrin, 1939), chap. viii, esp. pp. 220–222. For a general comparison between the God of Aristotle and the God of Saint Thomas Aquinas, see the penetrating essay of Anton C. Pegis, *Saint Thomas and*

lence, the act of all acts, is also a world wherein, for each and every thing, existence is the original energy whence flows all that which deserves the name of being. Such an existential world can be accounted for by no other cause than a supremely existential God. The strange thing is that, historically speaking, things seem to have worked the other way around. Philosophers have not inferred the supreme existentiality of God from any previous knowledge of the existential nature of things; on the contrary, the self-revelation of the existentiality of God has helped philosophers toward the realization of the existential nature of things. In other words, philosophers were not able to reach, beyond essences, the existential energies which are their very causes, until the Jewish-Christian Revelation had taught them that "to be" was the proper name of the Supreme Being. The decisive

the Greeks (Milwaukee, Marquette University Press, 1939). For a comparison between the God of Augustine and the God of Thomas Aquinas, see A. Gardeil, *La Structure de l'âme et l'expérience mystique* (Paris, Gabalda, 1927), Appendix II, vol. II, 313–325. The extreme simplicity of the notion of existence and the impossibility of our conceptualizing it have been stressed by J. Maritain, *Sept leçons sur l'Être (1932–33)* (Paris, Téqui), pp. 98–99. These characteristics of "to be" probably account for the fact that, as will be seen in Chapter IV, many modern scientists consider the existence of a thing the most negligible of all its properties.

progress achieved by metaphysics in the light of Christian faith has not been to realize that there must be a first being, cause of being in all things. The greatest among the Greeks already knew it. When, for instance, Aristotle was positing his first self-thinking Thought as the supreme being, he certainly conceived it as a pure Act and as an infinitely powerful energy; still, his god was but the pure Act of a Thought. This infinitely powerful actuality of a self-thinking principle most certainly deserves to be called a pure Act, but it was a pure Act in the order of knowing, not in that of existence. Now nothing can give what it has not. Because the supreme Thought of Aristotle was not "He who is," it could not give existence: hence the world of Aristotle was not a created world. Because the supreme Thought of Aristotle was not the pure Act of existing, its self-knowledge did not entail the knowledge of all being, both actual and possible: the god of Aristotle was not a providence; he did not even know a world which he did not make and which he could not possibly have made because he was the thought of a Thought, nor did he know the self-awareness of "Him who is."

I would not like to minimize the philosophical indebtedness of Thomas Aquinas to Aristotle. He himself would not forgive me for making him guilty of such an ingratitude. As a philosopher, Thomas Aquinas was not a pupil of Moses, but of Aristotle, to whom he owed his method, his principles, up to even his all-important notion of the fundamental actuality of being. My only point is that a decisive metaphysical progress or, rather, a true metaphysical revolution was achieved when somebody began to translate all the problems concerning being from the language of essences into that of existences. From its earliest origins, metaphysics had always obscurely aimed at becoming existential; from the time of Saint Thomas Aquinas it has always been so, and to such an extent that metaphysics has regularly lost its very existence every time it has lost its existentiality.

The metaphysics of Thomas Aquinas was, and it still remains, a climax in the history of natural theology. No wonder then that it was so soon followed by an anticlimax. Human reason feels at home in a world of things, whose essences and laws it can grasp and define in terms of concepts; but shy and ill at ease in a world of existences, because to exist is an act, not a thing. And we know it but too well. Every time a lecturer begins a sentence by saying: "As a matter of fact," you know at once that the man is at his wit's end. Granting that something is, he can tell you a great deal concerning that which it is; what he cannot do is to account for the very existence of the thing. How could he, if existence is a principle, and the innermost first principle of what the thing is? When dealing with facts as facts, or with things that happen as mere happenings, our *ultima ratio* always is and that's that. Obviously, to ask us to view the universe as a world of particular existential acts all related to a supreme and absolute Self-Existence is to stretch the power of our essentially conceptual reason almost to the breaking point. We know that we must do it, but we wonder if we can, because we are not sure that the thing can be done at all.

This, at least, is a point about which several among the successors of Thomas Aquinas have entertained grave doubts. Themselves Christian theologians, and sometimes very great ones, they had no hesitations concerning the true name of the true God. Their real difficulty was, granting that God is "He who is," can such a God be attained by means of philosophical reason alone, unaided by Revelation? A perfectly relevant question indeed. After all, these theologians knew full well that philosophers had never thought of giving God such a name until they had learned it from Moses, who himself had learned it from God. Hence the marked tendency, even in such a great metaphysician as Duns Scotus, to question the possibility of human reason's reaching, by means of philosophy alone, the absolutely existing and absolutely all-powerful Christian God.[17]

The reason for this hesitancy is simple. The human mind feels shy before a reality of which it can form no proper concept. Such, precisely, is existence. It is hard for us to realize that "I am" is an active verb. It is perhaps still more difficult for us to see that "it is" ultimately points out, not that which the thing is, but the primitive existential act which

17. The existential character of being has been powerfully stressed by Duns Scotus; cf. Parthenius Minges, *I. Duns Scoti Doctrina philosophica et theologica* (Firenze, Quaracchi, 1930), I, 14–17. What is peculiar to his own theology is a marked tendency to make the Christian God, taken *qua* Christian God, unknowable to natural reason unaided by faith. Moreover, it would prove interesting to investigate into the Scotist notion of created existence. According to him, "the essence and its existence in creatures are to each other as a quiddity to its mode" (*op. cit.*, pp. 16–17). The primacy of essence, which makes existence to be but one of its "accidents," appears in the doctrine of Duns Scotus as a remnant of the Platonism anterior to Thomas Aquinas. In a straight existential metaphysics, it would be much more correct to speak of the essence of an existence than to speak, with Duns Scotus, of the existence of an essence (*essentia et eius existentia*).

causes it both to be and to be precisely that which it is. He who begins to see this, however, also begins to grasp the very stuff our universe is made of. He even begins obscurely to perceive the supreme cause of such a world.

Why had the Greek mind spontaneously stopped at the notion of nature, or of essence, as at an ultimate explanation? Because, in our human experience, existence is always that of a particular essence. We directly know only individual and sensible existing things whose existence merely consists in being this and that individual thing. The existence of an oak tree obviously limits itself to being an oak tree or, rather, to being this one particular oak tree, and the same could be said of everything else. What does this mean, if not that the essence of any and every thing is not existence itself, but only one of the many possible sharings in existence? This fact is best expressed by the fundamental distinction of "being" and "what is" so clearly laid down by Thomas Aquinas. It does not mean that existence is distinct from essence as a thing from another thing. Once more, existence is not a thing, but the act that causes a thing both to be and to be what it is. This distinction merely expresses the fact that, in our human experience, there is no thing whose essence it is "to be," and not "to-be-a-certain-thing." The definition of no empirically given thing is existence; hence its essence is not existence, but existence must be conceived as distinct from it.

How then are we to account for the existence of a world made up of such things? You can take them all one after the other and ask yourself why each of them is, or exists; the essence of no one of them will ever yield the answer to your question. Since the nature of no one of them is "to be," the most exhaustive scientific knowledge of what they are will not so much as suggest the beginning of an answer to the question: Why are they? This world of ours is a world of change; physics, chemistry, biology can teach us the laws according to which change actually happens in it; what these sciences cannot teach us is why this world, taken together with its laws, its order, and its intelligibility, is, or exists. If the nature of no known thing is "to be," the nature of no known thing contains in itself the sufficient reason for its own existence. But it points to its sole conceivable cause. Beyond a world wherein "to be" is everywhere at hand, and where every nature can account for what other natures are but not for their common existence, there must be some cause whose very essence it is "to be." To posit such a being whose essence is a pure Act of existing, that is, whose essence is not to be this and that, but "to be," is also to posit the Christian God as the supreme cause of the universe. A most deeply hidden God, "He who is" is also a most obvious God. By revealing to the metaphysician that they cannot account for their own existence, all things point to the fact that there is such a supreme cause wherein essence and existence coincide. Here at last, Thomas Aquinas and Augustine ultimately meet. Because his own existential metaphysics has succeeded in forcing its way through that crust of essences which is but the outer coating of reality, Thomas Aquinas can see the pure Act of existing as one sees the presence of the cause in any one of its effects.

To reach this point was probably to reach the *ultima Thule* of the metaphysical world. Saint Augustine had reached it on the strength of Christian faith, on the very day he had heard all things proclaim, in the language of the Bible: "We created not ourselves, but were created by Him who abideth for ever." To Augustine, however, "He who abideth for ever" essentially remained the self-existing "eternal Truth, true Love and loved Eternity."[18] Saint Thomas Aquinas has reached it on the strength of straight metaphysical knowledge, where he says that "all knowing beings implicitly know God in any and every thing that they know."[19] It was impossible to go further, because human reason cannot go further than the highest of all metaphysical principles. One might have expected at least this, that once in possession of so fundamental a truth, men would carefully preserve it. But they did not. Its loss almost immediately followed its discovery. How and why it has been lost is therefore the problem to which we now have to turn our attention.

18. Saint Augustine, *Confessions,* Bk. X, chap. x, n. 25, English trans., p. 227. Cf. Bk. VII, chap. x, n. 16, p. 158.

19. Saint Thomas Aquinas, *Quaestiones disputatae de Veritate,* qu. 22, art. 2, ad 1^{m}. Similar statements will be found wherever Thomas Aquinas speaks about the natural and confused desire of all men for beatitude; for instance, *Summa theologica,* Pars I, qu. 2, art. 1, ad 1^{m}.

III

GOD AND MODERN PHILOSOPHY

THE transition from medieval philosophy to early modern philosophy is best illustrated by the change that took place in the social condition of the philosophers themselves. During the Middle Ages practically all the philosophers were monks, priests, or at least simple clerics. From the seventeenth century up to our own days very few churchmen have exhibited real creative genius in the field of philosophy. Malebranche and Condillac in France, Berkeley in Ireland, Rosmini in Italy can be quoted but as exceptions to the rule, and none of them is ever reckoned among the outstanding philosophical geniuses of modern times. Modern philosophy has been created by laymen, not by churchmen, and to the ends of the natural cities of men, not to the end of the supernatural city of God.

This epoch-making change became apparent when, in the First Part of his *Discourse upon Method*, Descartes announced his decision "to seek no other knowledge than that which" he "was able to find within" himself "or else in the great book of the world."[1] Descartes' statement did not mean at all that it was his intention to do away with God, with religion, or even with theology; but it emphatically meant that, in so far as he himself was concerned, such matters were not fitting objects for philosophical speculation. After all, is not the way to heaven open to the most ignorant as well as to the most learned? Does not the Church itself teach that the revealed truths which lead men to salvation lie beyond the reach of our intelligence? Let religion remain to us then what it actually is in itself: a matter of faith, not of intellectual knowledge or of rational demonstration.

What thus happened with the philosophy of Descartes, and quite independently from his personal Christian conviction, was the disruption of the medieval ideal of Christian Wisdom. To Saint Thomas Aquinas, for instance, the supreme expression of wisdom was theology. "This sacred doctrine," Thomas Aquinas says, "is wisdom par excellence among all the human wisdoms; it is not highest in a certain order only, but absolutely." And why is it so? Because the proper object

1. Descartes, *Discours de la méthode,* Première Partie, ed. Adam-Tannery, VI, 9, ll. 21–22.

of theology is God, who is the highest conceivable object of human knowledge: "He eminently deserves to be called wise, whose consideration is about the absolutely supreme cause of the universe, that is, God."[2] As the science of the supreme cause, theology reigns supreme among all the other sciences; they all are judged by it and subordinated to it. Against this wisdom of Christian faith, Descartes was no man to raise any objection. Himself a Christian, he looked at it as at his only means of personal salvation through Christ and the Church of Christ. As a philosopher, however, he was looking for an altogether different sort of wisdom, namely, a knowledge of truth by its first causes to be attained by natural reason alone and directed toward practical temporal ends.[3] Descartes did not differ from Saint Thomas Aquinas in that he suppressed theology—he very carefully preserved it; nor in that he formally distinguished philosophy from theology—Saint Thomas Aquinas had done it many centuries

2. Saint Thomas Aquinas, *Summa theologica,* Pars I, qu. 1, art. 6, *Resp.*

3. Descartes, *Principes de la philosophie,* Préface, ed. Adam-Tannery, Part II, Vol. IX, 4, ll. 19–23. Cf. p. 5, ll. 13–18. On this point, see J. Maritain, *Le Songe de Descartes* (Paris, R.-A. Corrêa, 1932), ch. iii, "Déposition de la sagesse," pp. 79–150.

before him. What was new with Descartes was his actual and practical separation of philosophical wisdom and theological wisdom. Whereas Thomas Aquinas distinguished in order to unite, Descartes divided in order to separate. Let the theologians take him to his supreme supernatural Good by means of the wisdom of faith; not only will Descartes have no objection, but he will feel exceedingly grateful. As he himself says: "As much as anyone, I strive to gain heaven."[4] As a philosopher, however, Descartes was after an entirely different sort of wisdom, that is, the rational knowledge "of the first causes and of the true principles whence the reasons of all that which it is possible to know can be deduced."[5] Such is the natural and human good, "considered by natural reason without the light of faith."

The immediate consequence of such an attitude should have been to bring back human reason to the philosophical attitude of the Greeks. Since Descartes' philosophy was neither directly nor indirectly regulated by

4. Descartes, *Discours de la méthode,* Première Partie, ed. Adam-Tannery, VI, 8, ll. 8–9. Exactly: "Je révérais notre théologie, et prétendais, autant qu'aucun autre, à gagner le ciel."

5. Descartes, *Principes de la philosophie,* Préface, p. 5, ll. 21–24.

theology, he had no reason whatsoever to suppose that their conclusions would ultimately coincide. Why should there not have been between the object, or objects, of his religious worship and the rational principle of intelligibility of all things the same separation there was between his faith and his reason, or his theology and his philosophy? It would have been so logical for Descartes to adopt such a position that some of his best historians do not hesitate to maintain that in fact he did. In O. Hamelin's own words: "Descartes comes after the Ancients almost as though there had been nothing else between him and them, save only the physicists."[6]

That, logically speaking, this is what should have happened, is beyond a doubt. That, however, nothing of the sort did actually happen is also beyond a doubt, and the fact is susceptible of a very simple historical explanation. When a Greek philosopher had to approach the problem of natural theology by a purely rational method, he found himself confronted only with the religious gods of Greek mythology. Whatever his name, his rank, or function, not one among the gods of Greek religion had ever claimed to be the one,

6. O. Hamelin, *Le Systême de Descartes* (2d ed., Paris, Alcan, 1921), p. 15.

sole, and supreme Being, creator of the world, first principle, and ultimate end of all things. Descartes, on the contrary, could not approach the same philosophical problem without finding himself confronted with the Christian God. When a philosopher is also a Christian, he can very well say, at the beginning of his inquiry: Let me pretend that I am not a Christian; let me try to seek, by reason alone and without the light of faith, the first causes and the first principles whereby all things can be explained. As an intellectual sport, this is as good as any other one; but it is bound to result in a failure, because when a man both knows and believe that there is but one cause of all that is, the God in whom he believes can hardly be other than the cause which he knows.

The whole problem of modern natural theology is there in a nutshell, and to realize its paradoxical nature is the first condition for a correct understanding of its history. Far from coming after the Greeks as though there had been nothing in between, Descartes has come after the Greeks with the naïve condition that he could solve, by the purely rational method of the Greeks, all the problems which had been raised in between by Christian natural theology. In other words, Descartes never doubted for a single moment that the first principle of a philosophy wholly separated from Christian theology would finally prove to be the very same God whom philosophy had never been able to discover so long as it had remained foreign to the influence of Christian revelation. No wonder then that we historians do not agree on Descartes. Some of us write the history of what he said; some others write the history of what he actually did; and just as he said that he would seek truth in the light of reason alone, what he did, at least in metaphysics, was to restate the main conclusions of Christian natural theology as if Christian supernatural theology itself had never existed. To Liard, Descartes appears as the pioneer of scientific positivism; to Espinas, he appears as a faithful pupil of his first professors, the Jesuits.[7] In fact, Descartes was both, and both at one and the same time, but not with regard to the same questions.

The God of Descartes is an unmistakably Christian God. The common foundation for

7. Descartes has been interpreted by Victor Cousin as an exponent of his own spiritualistic metaphysics. Against this predominantly metaphysical interpretation of his doctrine, the scientific elements of Cartesianism have been stressed by L. Liard, *Descartes* (Paris, Alcan, 1882); later, under the influence of L. Lévy-Bruhl's unpublished lectures, by myself, in *La Liberté chez Descartes et la théologie* (Paris, Alcan, 1913). The whole problem has been reconsidered, and my own conclusions

the Cartesian demonstrations of the existence of such a God is the clear and distinct idea of a thinking, uncreated, and independent substance, which is naturally innate within the human mind. If we investigate into the cause why such an idea exists within us, we are at once led to posit, as the only conceivable explanation for it, a being who is possessed of all the attributes which attend our own idea of him, that is, a self-existing, infinite, all-powerful, one and unique being. But it is enough for us directly to consider our innate idea of him, to make sure that God is, or exists. We are so accustomed, in all other things, to make a distinction between essence and existence, that we naturally feel inclined to imagine that God can be conceived as not actually existent. Nevertheless, when we think more attentively of God, we soon find that the nonexistence of God is, strictly speaking, unthinkable. Our innate idea of God is that of a

ably corrected, by Henri Gouhier, *La Pensée religieuse de Descartes* (Paris, J. Vrin, 1924). During the same years when Lévy-Bruhl was teaching his scientific-minded Descartes, an apologetics-minded Descartes was being elaborated by A. Espinas. The result of his reflections is to be found in Espinas' posthumous book, *Descartes et la morale* (Paris, 1925), 2 vols. The latest discussion of the problem is to be found in the book of Francesco Olgiati, *Cartesio, Vita e Pensiero* (Milano, 1934).

supremely perfect being; since existence is a perfection, to think of a supremely perfect being to whom existence is wanting is to think of a supremely perfect being to whom some perfection is wanting, which is contradictory; hence existence is inseparable from God and, consequently, he necessarily is, or exists.[8]

It is a well-known fact that Descartes always despised history; but here history has paid him back in full. Had he ever so little investigated into the past of his own idea of God, he would have realized at once that though it be true that all men have a certain idea of the divinity, they have not all, or always, had the Christian idea of God. If all men had such an idea of God, Moses would not have asked Jehovah for his name; or else Jehovah's answer would have been: "What a silly question! You know it." Descartes was so anxious not to corrupt the rational purity of his metaphysics by any admixture of Christian faith that he simply decreed the universal innateness of the Christian definition of God. Like the innate Ideas of Plato, Descartes' innate idea of God was a reminiscence; not, however, the reminiscence of some idea contemplated by the soul in a former life, but

8. Descartes, *Méditations,* V, ed. Adam-Tannery, IX, 52.

simply the reminiscence of what he had learned in church when he was a little boy.

This disconcerting indifference of Descartes toward the possible origin of so important a metaphysical idea is by no means a unique accident in his philosophy. Of the many things which had been said by his predecessors, a large number appeared to him as being at least materially true, and Descartes never hesitated to repeat them when it suited him to do so. To him, however, to repeat something never meant to borrow it. As Descartes himself saw it, the greatest merit of his own philosophy consisted in this, that because it was the first one to have consistently followed the only true method, it also was the only one to be a continuous chain of demonstrated consequences faultlessly drawn from evident principles. Just change, I do not say one of the rings, but merely its place, and the whole chain goes to pieces.[9] Where the truth value of an idea is so wholly inseparable from its place in the order of deduction, why should one worry about its origin? There is but one place where a true idea is fully true; it is the very place it finds in Descartes' own philosophy. And the Cartesian idea of God is an

9. Descartes, *Principes de la philosophie,* Préface, IX, 19, ll. 12–26.

outstanding application of this principle. Assuredly it is the keystone of Descartes' metaphysics, but since human wisdom is one, there is no such thing as an isolated Cartesian metaphysics. What is the keystone of Cartesian metaphysics must of necessity also be the keystone of the physics which borrows its principles from metaphysics. In short, what gave to his idea of God its full value in the mind of Descartes was its remarkable aptness to become the starting point of a purely scientific interpretation of the world. Because the Cartesian God was metaphysically true, he provided science with the principles of true physics, and because no other one could provide true physics with the principles it needs for a systematic exposition, no other God but the Cartesian God could possibly be the true God.

This must be carefully kept in mind by anybody who wishes to understand the curious metaphysical adventures of Descartes' God. By origin, he was the Christian God. Not only was he a Being as wholly self-subsisting as the God of Saint Thomas Aquinas himself, but Descartes would gladly have made him even more so, if the thing had been possible at all. His own God was not simply a pure Act of existing which had no cause for his own existence; he was like an infinite energy of self-existence which, so to speak, was to itself the cause of its own existence. Of course, there are no words to describe such a God. Since a cause naturally appears to us as distinct from its effect, it is awkward to speak of him as if he were his own cause. Yet, could we bring the two notions of cause and effect to coincide, at least in this unique case, an infinitely powerful self-causing Being would perhaps be the least inadequate of all the human approximations of God.[10]

At first sight, the God of Descartes and the God of Saint Thomas Aquinas do not seem to differ by more than a shade of metaphysical thought. But there is more in this than meets the eye. When Thomas Aquinas had transfigured the supreme Thought of Aristotle into the Christian "He who is," he had raised a first philosophical principle up to the level of God. Starting from this very same Christian God, Descartes was now using him as a first philosophical principle. True enough, the God in whom, as a Christian, Descartes believed was the selfsame God whom, as a phi-

10. For a detailed discussion of this notion of God and of the texts of Descartes where it is formulated, see É. Gilson, *Études sur le rôle de la pensée médiévale dans la formation du systême cartésien* (Paris, J. Vrin, 1930).

losopher, he knew to be the supreme cause of all things; the fact however remains that, as a philosopher, Descartes had no use for God taken in himself and in his absolute self-sufficient perfection. To him God in himself was an object of religious faith; what was an object of rational knowledge was God taken as the highest among the "Principles of Philosophy." This is the reason why the natural theology of Descartes not only limited itself to the consideration of those among the divine attributes that account for the existence of the world but also conceived these attributes as they have to be conceived in order to account for the existence of a Cartesian world.

What the Cartesian world of science was everybody knows. It is an exclusively mechanical universe, wherein everything can be accounted for by the geometrical properties of space and the physical laws of motion.[11] If we look at God as the only possible explanation for the existence of such a world, his main attribute must necessarily be not the self-contemplation of his own infinite Being, but his self-causing all-powerfulness, source of his creative causality. Instead of the self-suffi-

11. Descartes, *op. cit.*, Deuxième Partie, IX, chap. lxiv, 101–102.

cient and self-knowing Being of Thomas Aquinas, we now have a self-causing energy of existence. Were we to resort to metaphors, we might say that whereas the God of Saint Thomas was an infinite ocean of existence, the God of Descartes is an infinitely powerful fountain of existence. And it is not difficult to see why. Since the ultimate philosophical function of his God was to be a cause, the Cartesian God had to be possessed of any and every attribute which was required of the creator of a Cartesian world. Such a world being indefinitely extended in space, its creator had to be infinite; such a world being purely mechanical and devoid of final causes, what was true and good in it had to be such because God had created it by a free decree of his will, and not conversely; the mechanical world of Descartes rested upon the assumption of the conservation of the same quantity of motion in the universe; hence the God of Descartes had to be an immutable God and the laws established by his will could not be allowed to change, unless this world itself be first destroyed. In short, the essence of the Cartesian God was largely determined by his philosophical function, which was to create and to preserve the mechanical world of science as Descartes himself conceived it.[12] Now it is quite true that a Creator is an eminently Christian God, but a God whose very essence is to be a creator is not a Christian God at all. The essence of the true Christian God is not to create but to be. "He who is" can also create, if he chooses; but he does not exist because he creates, nay, not even himself; he can create because he supremely is.

We are now beginning to see why, and in what sense, the metaphysics of Descartes was a decisive moment in the evolution of natural theology. Evolution, however, is not always synonymous with progress; and this time it was destined to be a regress. I am not arguing

12. Hence the justly famous remark of Pascal: "I cannot forgive Descartes. In all his philosophy he would have been quite willing to dispense with God. But he had to make Him give a fillip to set the world in motion; beyond this, he had no further need of God." *Pascal's Pensées,* trans. W. F. Trotter, pp. 153–154, Everyman's Library. This physicism, or naturalism, which pervades the natural theology of Descartes, has been keenly observed and admirably analyzed by Maurice Blondel, "L'Anti-cartésianisme de Malebranche," in *Revue de métaphysique et de morale,* 1916, pp. 1–26. The only addition I would like to make to this most excellent essay is that Malebranche has tried to express his own anticartesian spirit in terms of Cartesian philosophy. Hence his personal difficulties. In his effort to re-Christianize the natural theology of Descartes, Malebranche has Cartesianized the Christian God.

here on the dogmatic assumption that the God of Saint Thomas is the true God. What I am trying to make clear is the objective fact that, even as a philosophical supreme cause, the God of Descartes was a stillborn God. He could not possibly live because, as Descartes had conceived him, he was the God of Christianity reduced to the condition of philosophical principle, in short, an infelicitous hybrid of religious faith and of rational thought. The most striking characteristic of such a God was that his creative function had integrally absorbed his essence. Hence, the name that was hereafter going to be his truest name: no longer "He who is" but rather "The Author of Nature." Assuredly, the God of Christianity had always been the Author of Nature, but he had always been infinitely more than that, whereas, after Descartes, he was destined progressively to become nothing else than that. Descartes himself was too good a Christian to consider Nature as a particular god; but, strangely enough, it never occurred to him that to reduce the Christian God himself to no more than the supreme cause of Nature was to do identically the same thing. Metaphysical conclusions so necessarily follow from their principles that Descartes himself reached at once what were to be the ultimate conclusions of his eighteenth-century disciples when he wrote the following sentence: "By Nature, considered in general, I am now understanding nothing else than either God, or the order and the disposition established by God in created things."[13]

The most immediate historical effect of this Cartesian natural theology has been again to dissociate God as an object of religious worship from God as a first principle of philosophical intelligibility. Hence the famous protest of Pascal: "The God of Christians is not a God who is simply the author of mathematical truths, or of the order of the elements; that is the view of heathens and Epicureans . . . ; but the God of Abraham, the God of Isaac, the God of Jacob, the God of Christians, is a God of love and of comfort, a God who fills the soul and heart of those whom he possesses."[14] In a sense it can be said that the greatest among the immediate successors of Descartes did all that was humanly conceivable to restore the unity of natural theology on the basis of Cartesian principles. If they

13. Descartes, *Méditations,* VI, ed. Adam-Tannery, IX, 64.

14. *Pascal's Pensées,* pp. 153–154.

failed, as I am afraid they did, the reason for their failure probably was that such an undertaking was in itself a contradictory one and, consequently, that the thing could not be done at all.

Had it been possible successfully to achieve such a task, Malebranche would have been the most likely man to do it. Himself a priest of the Oratory, a deeply pious man, almost a mystic, Malebranche combined in his own person all the conditions required in order to succeed in this philosophical experiment. As a physicist, he felt perfectly satisfied with the mechanical principles laid down by Descartes; as a metaphysician, he had worked out an original synthesis of Cartesianism and Augustinianism which posited God as the sole source of causal efficacy both in the order of human knowledge and in the order of physical causality; as a theologian, he would maintain that God always acts in conformity with that which He is and that the only end of God in His action is His own glory in the person of Jesus Christ. What is God, Malebranche asks, if not Being itself? "I think I understand you correctly," Ariste says in one of Malebranche's dialogues, "you are defining God just as, speaking to Moses, He has defined Himself:

God is the One who Is."[15] Is not this, one may ask, the truly and genuinely Christian God?

It no doubt is. An infinitely perfect Being, the God of Malebranche "is to Himself His own light, He discovers in His own substance the essences of all beings and all their possible modalities, and, in His decrees, their existence as well as all their actual modalities."[16] There is not a single word in this definition that would not apply just as well to the God of Saint Thomas Aquinas. Far from conceding to Descartes that God freely creates eternal truths, Malebranche restores in full the Augustinian doctrine of a God who knows all things, both actual and possible, by knowing his own eternal Ideas, and who knows his Ideas by knowing his own substance. Here, however, is the loose joint, where the Cartesian spirit has leaked into the natural theology of Malebranche. In a way, a God who sees nothing but in his own substance, and who there sees all beings together with all

15. Malebranche, *Entretiens sur la métaphysique et sur la religion,* ed. Paul Fontana (A. Colin, 1922), Vol. I, chap. ii, sec. 4, p. 46. For a general exposition of Malebranche's doctrine, see Henri Gouhier, *La Vocation de Malebranche* (Paris, J. Vrin, 1926), and *La Philosophie de Malebranche et son expérience religieuse* (Paris, J. Vrin, 1926).

16. Malebranche, *Entretiens sur la métaphysique et sur la religion,* Vol. I, chap. viii, sec. 10, p. 182.

their intelligible relations, is the very reverse of the God of Descartes. But, curiously enough, the difference between these two Gods is due to the fact that Malebranche has thoroughly Cartesianized the, to him, insufficiently Cartesian God of Descartes. The world of Descartes had been a world of intelligible laws established by the arbitrary will of an all-powerful God; Malebranche's originality was to conceive God himself as an infinite world of intelligible laws. Nothing more closely resembles the supreme Intellect of Plotinos than the divine Word of Malebranche. Many historians would say they are the same. At any rate, they are so much alike that one might almost define the Word of Malebranche as a Plotinian Intellect which has turned Cartesian. In short, with Malebranche, the Creator himself has to submit to the very type of intelligibility which the God of Descartes had freely imposed upon created things.

The net result of Malebranche's metaphysical venture has been the rise of a supernatural God whose inner life was conceived after the pattern of a Cartesian world. By simply knowing in himself all his possible finite participations, the God of Malebranche knows all conceivable beings and all their conceivable relations. He knows all their quantitative relations as comprised within his single and simple idea of the intelligible extension. In other words, the physics of God is the same as that of Descartes. And how could it be otherwise? Since the only true world is the geometrical world of Descartes, where everything can be accounted for by the sole properties of extension in space, God himself can know and create matter but through the intelligible idea of extension. Since all speculative truths bear upon relations of extension, the world of matter is known by God, just as Descartes himself thought he knew it, through this simple knowledge of all the possible relations of extension.

How then are we to account for the fact that, among the infinite number of possible systems of relations in space, God singled out precisely the one we live in, in order to create it? Malebranche's answer to this question is that, besides the relations of quantity, there are relations of perfection. Two and two make four is a relation in the order of quantity; man is superior to beasts is a relation in the order of perfection. Now, just as quantitative relations are purely speculative in kind, relations of perfection are practical by definition. What appears to us as better is that which appears to us as more lovable. So is it with

God. Taken together, all the possible relations of perfection between all the possible beings form an infinite system, which we call Order. Now "God invincibly loves this immutable Order, which consists, and can consist, but in the relations of perfection there are between his own attributes, as well as between the ideas that are comprised within his own substance." God then could not love, or will, anything that contradicts this eternal and absolute Order without loving and willing against his own perfection, which is impossible.[17] This is why God has created this one world such as it is. It is not, absolutely speaking, the most perfect possible world, but it is at least the most perfect world which God could possibly create, given that it had to be a world ruled by universal, uniform, and intelligible laws.[18] A congeries of individually perfect things would not be a whole, nor would it be a world, because it would not be an order of things regulated by laws.

Perhaps the best way for us to understand the God of Malebranche is to ask ourselves this question: Granting that the Cartesian world is the most intelligible of all possible worlds, why has God singled out just that one

17. *Ibid.*, Vol. I, chap. viii, sec. 13, pp. 185–187.
18. *Ibid.*, Vol. II, chap. ix, sec. 10, pp. 209–211.

in order to create it? To which the answer naturally is because God is supremely intelligent, he could not fail to do what Descartes would have done, had Descartes been God. Strikingly enough, this is exactly how Descartes himself had asked the question at the beginning of his unfinished treatise on "The World"; not at all: What is this universe made of? but rather: Supposing we had to create out of nothing a perfectly rational universe, how would we go at it? Malebranche did nothing more than to go one step further along the same road. To the question: Could God have created another universe? the answer of Saint Thomas had been: Yes, certainly; since God is perfect, the world which he has created is very good, but he could have created many different good ones, and why, among these many possible universes, he has singled out this one to grant it existence, we don't know: He is free. Malebranche, too, had always maintained that God was eternally free to create or not to create; but he added that, since God had freely chosen to create, his own perfection bound him to create the best world is was possible for a God acting as becomes a perfect God to create.

Clearly enough, the notion of perfection is here taking precedence over the notion of being. Malebranche still calls God, Being; in fact, however, and under the dominant influence of Augustine, he conceives him like the Good of Plotinos and of Plato. Now, even the Good is an essence, or nature, and there is a vast difference between saying that God cannot not exist because he is perfect, and saying that God cannot not be perfect because he is "He who is." Malebranche says the second but he thinks the first. Consequently, this most pious disciple of Saint Augustine unconsciously goes back to the awkward position which had been that of his master thirteen centuries before him: he has not the natural philosophy of his revealed theology; the God of his philosophy is not the same as the God of his religion.

There is nothing surprising in such a fact. In so far as his philosophical method was concerned, Malebranche was a Cartesian. One of the deepest exigencies, and probably the deepest exigency, of the Cartesian method is never to go from things to ideas, but on the contrary from ideas to things. Existences are given to a Cartesian only through, and in, essences. God himself could not be posited as actually existing were it not for the fact that his idea is in us, and that, as it is found there, it involves existence. As the Descartes of the fifth

Meditation explicitly says: since we cannot possibly separate existence from the idea of God, God necessarily is, or exists. Despite the shades of thought that are proper to his own system, Malebranche's position has remained substantially the same: "One cannot see the essence of the Infinite without its existence, the idea of Being without being."[19] Such also, and for the same reason, was the position of Leibniz, whose favorite proof of the existence of God posits him as the only conceivable cause of the essences, and therefore as the necessary Being whose essence includes existence, "or in whom possibility is sufficient to produce actuality." One could hardly wish for a more perfect formula of the primacy of essence over existence: "God alone, or the Necessary Being, has this prerogative, that if he be possible [that is: if his essence be conceivable without contradiction] he must necessarily exist."[20]

If one keeps in mind that God is that Being whose very possibility produces his actuality, he will not feel surprised to learn that the world created by such a God is also the only

19. *Ibid.*, Vol. I, chap. ii, sec. 5, p. 47.

20. Leibniz, *Monadology*, nn. 44, 45; English trans. by G. R. Montgomery, in *Discourse on Metaphysics, Correspondence with Arnauld and Monadology* (2d ed., The Open Court Co., 1918), p. 258.

one which such a God could possibly have created. The best definition of the Leibnizian God is an absolutely perfect being.[21] As such, the God of Leibniz is also to be an infinitely generous God; and because, morally speaking at least, he can hardly refrain from communicating his own perfection, he has to create. Now a perfect God can create only the best possible world. Among the infinite series of possible worlds, the best one obviously will be the one wherein the highest conceivable richness of effects will be achieved by the simplest possible means. As Leibniz himself says, this is what the mathematicians call a problem of *maximum* and *minimum*. Such problems are susceptible of but one solution. Consequently, the best possible world is exactly the one we are in.[22] A most gratifying certitude indeed, at least so long as it lasts, and Voltaire was to see to it that it did not outlive the earthquake of Lisbon. The metaphysical difficulty however was not there; it rather lay in the fact that Leibniz pretended to make us accept as the supreme Being a God who was but a nature. As a matter of fact, the God of the *Monadology* was but the Good of Plato, solving the problem of which world to create, by

21. Leibniz, *Discourse on Metaphysics,* chap. i, p. 3.
22. *Ibid.,* chap. v, pp. 8–9.

means of the infinitesimal calculus recently discovered by Leibniz.

The greatest metaphysician among the successors of Descartes was Spinoza, because, with him, somebody at last said about God what Descartes himself, if not as a Christian, at least as a philosopher, should have thought and said from the very beginning. Descartes had been either religiously right and philosophically wrong, or philosophically right and religiously wrong; Spinoza has been wholly right or wholly wrong, either philosophically or religiously. Spinoza had neither the religion of a Christian nor that of a Jew; having no religion whatsoever, he could not be expected to have the philosophy of any religion; but he was a thoroughbred philosopher, which accounts for the fact that he at least has had the religion of his philosophy. His God is an absolutely infinite being, or substance, which is "cause of itself" because its "essence involves existence."[23] The primacy of essence is here so forcefully stressed that nobody can miss its metaphysical significance. In the doctrine of Descartes, one may still

23. *Spinoza's Ethics,* Part I, definitions 1 and 6, English trans., p. 1, Everyman's Library. On Spinoza's philosophy, see Victor Delbos, *Le Spinozisme* (Paris, Société Française d'Imprimerie et de Librairie, 1916).

wonder if God's essence involves his existence in himself, or in our own mind only; in the *Ethics* of Spinoza, no hesitation remains possible. Just as a square circle cannot exist because its essence is a contradictory one, God cannot not exist because, in Spinoza's own words, "the existence of substance *follows from its nature alone*, for that involves existence."[24] Let us therefore conceive a universe wherein the existence of any and every thing expresses but the power to exist which belongs to its nature; only one being can be there posited as necessarily existing; it is God, or the being absolutely infinite, which, because it "has an infinite power of existence from itself," absolutely is, or exists.[25] But a God who "exists and acts merely from the necessity of his nature,"[26] is nothing more than a nature. Rather he is nature itself: *Deus sive Natura*.[27] God is the absolute essence whose intrinsic necessity makes necessary the being of all that is, so that he is absolutely all that is, just as, in as much as it is, all that is "necessarily involves the eternal and infinite essence of God."[28]

24. *Spinoza's Ethics,* Part I, prop. 11, p. 8.
25. *Ibid.,* p. 9.
26. *Ibid.,* Part I, Appendix, p. 30.
27. *Ibid.,* Part IV, Preface, p. 142.
28. *Ibid.,* Part II, prop. 45, p. 72.

Spinoza has often been branded as an atheist by his adversaries; he has also been called, by one of his German admirers, "a man inebriated with God."[29] What renders Spinoza so important in the history of natural theology is that both judgments are true. A religious atheist, Spinoza was truly inebriated with his philosophical God.[30] Positive religions as he saw them were but anthropomorphic superstitions invented by men for practical and political purposes. It is no wonder that, to Jews as well as to Christians, he always appeared as a godless man. But we must not forget the other side of the picture. As a philosopher, and toward his own philosophical God, Spinoza probably is the most pious thinker there ever was. Marcus Aurelius and Plato could perhaps compete with him for the title; but Plato had never gone so far as to worship the Good, and as for Marcus Aurelius' religion, it had never been more than his acceptance of an order of things which he could not change. Spinoza could do much more than accept nature; by thoroughly under-

29. Novalis.

30. On Spinoza's criticism of positive religions, see his *Theologico-Political Treatise,* and, before anything else, the unambiguous and outspoken statement of his position in his *Ethics,* Part I, Appendix, pp. 30–36.

standing it as an absolutely intelligible reality, he was progressively liberating himself from illusion, error, evil, mental slavery, and achieving that supreme human beatitude which is inseparable from spiritual liberty. I, personally, would not speak lightly of Spinoza's religion. It is a one hundred per cent metaphysically pure answer to the question how to achieve human salvation by means of philosophy only. I am well aware of the fact that what I myself hold as the true religion, that is, Christianity, appeared to him but a piece of childish mythology. But I feel infinitely grateful to him because, after having discarded all positive religion as purely mythological, he did not replace it by a philosophical mythology of his own. Spinoza is a Jew who turned "Him who is" into a mere "that which is"; and he could love "that which is," but he never expected that he himself would be loved by it. The only way for us to overcome Spinoza is, in a truly Spinozistic way, to free ourselves from his limitation by understanding it as a limitation. This means, to grasp again Being as the existence of essence, not as the essence of existence; to touch it as an act, not to conceive it as a thing. Spinoza's metaphysical experiment is the conclusive demonstration of at least this: That any religious God whose true name is not "He who is" is nothing but a myth.

One of the most delectable objects of contemplation for the connoisseurs of human silliness is precisely the myth which seems to have haunted so many minds from the middle of the seventeenth century up to the end of the eighteenth. "Haunted" is here the correct word, for this curious myth was but the philosophical ghost of the Christian God. The Deists, whose history has been several times ably sketched but never written in full, have always been considered by Christians as being at bottom simple atheists. "Deism," Bossuet says, "that is, Atheism in disguise."[31] A somewhat oversimplified statement of the case but nevertheless a true one, at least in so far as the God of any positive religion was concerned. The Deists were in full agreement with Spinoza on the fabulous character of any so-called revealed God. On the other side, and their very name shows it, they themselves had a God, but though they were most emphatic on the fact that he was a naturally known God, they did not at all conceive him as the philosophers had done. The God of the Deists

31. J. B. Bossuet, *The History of the Variations of the Protestant Churches,* Bk. V, chap. xxxi.

was not a first intelligible principle like the Good of Plato, the self-thinking Thought of Aristotle, or the Infinite Substance of Spinoza. The God of the Deists, as Dryden describes him in his famous Epistle, *Religio Laici; or, a Layman's Fate*, was a supreme Being, universally worshiped by all men in the same way, by the sole rules of Praise and Pray; yet a God Who could be offended by crime, and Who, when men sinned, expected them to atone for their faults by repentance; last, not least, their God was a God Whose justice had ultimately to be satisfied, if not in this life, then in another, where the good will reap reward, the bad punishment.[32]

Dryden himself was not a Deist, but his description of their doctrine was correct; and what was their doctrine if not this curious

32. Deism is at least as old as the sixteenth century. In his *Instruction Chrétienne* (1563), the Calvinist divine Viret criticizes people who believe in God but not in Christ, and according to whom the teachings of the Gospels are just so many fables. On English Deism, see the article "Christianisme rationnel," in *Dictionnaire de théologie catholique,* Vol. II, col. 2415–2417. A good introduction to the problem of Deism in general is the article "Déisme," in the same dictionary, Vol. IV, col. 232–243; bibliography, col. 243. For a more scholarly discussion of the problem, see Max Frischeisen-Köhler and Willy Moog, *Die Philosophie der Neuzeit bis zum Ende des XVIII. Jahrhunderts* (Berlin, 1924), pp. 376–380; bibliography, pp. 688–689.

sample of mental teratology, a natural Christianity? The very title of the famous book published in 1696 by John Toland contained the whole of Deism in a nutshell; I was about to say that title should have become the Deist's slogan: *Christianity Not Mysterious.* Toland's book was burned by the hangman at Dublin in 1697, but the natural theology of Deism, just as it had preceded the publication of the book, survived its condemnation. Represented in England by many writers, Herbert of Cherbury (1581–1648), Charles Blount (1654–1693), and Matthew Tindal (1653–1733), it dominated the French eighteenth century with men as widely different as Voltaire and Rousseau, until the cult of the Supreme Being was officially established by Robespierre at the time of the French Revolution.

I know of no greater tribute ever paid to the God of Christianity than His survival in this idea, maintained against Christianity itself and on the strength of pure natural reason. For almost two centuries—for I myself could quote French Deists whom I have personally known—this ghost of the Christian God has been attended by the ghost of Christian religion: a vague feeling of religiosity, a sort of trusting familiarity with some supremely good fellow to whom other good fellows can hopefully apply when they are in trouble: *le Dieu des bonnes gens.* As an object of religious worship, however, the God of the Deists was but the wraith of the living God of Abraham, of Isaac, and of Jacob. As an object of pure philosophical speculation, he was little more than a myth whose death sentence had been irrevocably passed by Spinoza. Having forgotten, together with "Him who is," the true meaning of the problem of existence, Fontenelle, Voltaire, Rousseau, and so many others with them had naturally to fall back upon the most superficial interpretation of the problem of final causes. God then became the "watchmaker" of Fontenelle and of Voltaire, the supreme engineer of the huge machine which this world is. In short, God became again what he had already been in the *Timaeus* of Plato: a Demiurge, the only difference being that this time, before beginning to arrange his world, the Demiurge had consulted Newton. Just like the Demiurge of Plato, the God of the Deists was but a philosophical myth. Strangely enough, what our own contemporaries are still asking themselves is whether this myth actually exists or not? Their answer is that it does not. And our contemporaries are right in giving the question such an answer; but the fact that there is no Demiurge does not prove that there is no God.

IV

GOD AND CONTEMPORARY THOUGHT

THE present-day position of the problem of God is wholly dominated by the thought of Immanuel Kant and of Auguste Comte. Their doctrines are about as widely different as two philosophical doctrines can possibly be. Yet the Criticism of Kant and the Positivism of Comte have this in common, that in both doctrines the notion of knowledge is reduced to that of scientific knowledge, and the notion of scientific knowledge itself to the type of intelligibility provided by the physics of Newton. The verb "to know" then means to express observable relations between given facts in terms of mathematical relations.[1] Now, however we look at it, no given fact answers to our notion of God. Since God is not an object of empirical knowledge, we have no concept of him. Consequently God is no object of knowledge, and what we call natural theology is just idle talking.

1. For a general introduction to the criticism of metaphysics by Kant and Comte, see É. Gilson, *The Unity of Philosophical Experience* (New York, Scribner, 1937), Part III, pp. 223–295.

If we compare it with the Kantian revolution, the Cartesian revolution hardly deserved such a name. From Thomas Aquinas to Descartes the distance is assuredly a long one. Yet, although extremely far from each other, they are on comparable lines of thought. Between Kant and them, the line has been broken. Coming after the Greeks, the Christian philosophers had asked themselves the question: How obtain from Greek metaphysics an answer to the problems raised by the Christian God? After centuries of patient work, one of them had at last found the answer, and that is why we find Thomas Aquinas constantly using the language of Aristotle in order to say Christian things. Coming after the Christian philosophers, Descartes, Leibniz, Malebranche, and Spinoza found themselves confronted with this new problem: How find a metaphysical justification for the world of seventeenth-century science? As scientists, Descartes and Leibniz had no metaphysics of their own. Just as Augustine and Thomas Aquinas had had to borrow their technique from the Greeks, Descartes and Leibniz had to borrow their technique from the Christian philosophers who had preceded them. Hence the vast number of scholastic expressions which we meet in the works of Descartes, Leibniz,

Spinoza, and even Locke. All of them freely use the language of the Schoolmen in order to express nonscholastic views of a nonscholastic world. Yet all of them appear to us as seeking in a more or less traditional metaphysics the ultimate justification of the mechanical world of modern science. In short, and this is true of Newton himself, the supreme principle of the intelligibility of nature remains, for all of them, the Author of Nature, that is, God.[2]

With the Criticism of Kant and the Positivism of Comte, things become entirely different. Since God is not an object apprehended in the a priori forms of sensibility, space and time, he cannot be related to anything else by the category of causality. Hence, Kant concludes, God may well be a pure idea of reason, that is, a general principle of unification of our cognitions; he is not an object of cognition. Or we may have to posit his existence as required by the exigencies of practical reason; the existence of God then becomes a postulate, it is still not a cognition. In his own way, which was a much more radical one, Comte at once reached identically the same conclusion. Science,

2. For a contemporary discussion of the scientific notion of cause, see Émile Meyerson, *Identité et réalité* (2d ed., Paris, Alcan, 1912), p. 42. *De l'explication dans les sciences* (Paris, Alcan, 1921), I, 57; *Essais* (Paris, J. Vrin, 1936), pp. 28–58.

Comte says, has no use for the notion of cause. Scientists never ask themselves *why* things happen, but *how* they happen. Now as soon as you substitute the positivist's notion of relation for the metaphysical notion of cause, you at once lose all right to wonder *why* things are, and why they are what they are. To dismiss all such questions as irrelevant to the order of positive knowledge is, at the same time, to cut the very root of all speculation concerning the nature and existence of God.

It had taken Christian thinkers thirteen centuries to achieve a perfectly consistent philosophy of the universe of Christianity. It has taken modern scientists about two centuries to achieve a perfectly consistent philosophy of the mechanical universe of modern science. This is a fact which it is very important for us to realize, because it clearly shows where the pure philosophical positions are actually to be found.

If what we are after is a rational interpretation of the world of science given as an ultimate fact, either the Criticism of Kant himself or some edition of his Criticism revised to suit the demands of today's science should provide us with a satisfactory answer to our question. We might nevertheless prefer the Positivism of Comte, or some revised edition of it. A large number among our own contemporaries actually subscribe to one or the other of these two possible attitudes. The Neo-Criticism has been represented by such men as Paulsen and Vaihinger in Germany, by Renouvier in France; and it has found what will perhaps remain its purest formulation in the works of our own contemporary, Professor Leon Brunschvicg. As to Positivism, it has found important supporters in England, John Stuart Mill and Herbert Spencer, for instance; in France, Émile Littré, Émile Durkheim, and the whole French sociological school; and it has recently been revived, under a new form, by the Neo-Positivism of the Vienna school. Whatever their many differences, all these schools have at least this in common, that their ambition does not extend beyond achieving a rational interpretation of the world of science given as an irreducible and ultimate fact.

But if we do not think that science is adequate to rational knowledge,[3] if we hold that other than scientifically answerable problems

3. A critical discussion of this unduly restricted notion of rational knowledge is to be found in J. Maritain, *The Degrees of Knowledge* (New York, Scribner, 1938); and also in W. R. Thompson, F.R.S., *Science and Common Sense, an Aristotelian Excursion* (New York, Longmans, Green, 1937), pp. 47–50.

can still be rationally posed concerning the universe, then there is no use for us to stop at the eighteenth-century Author of Nature. Why should we content ourselves with the ghost of God when we can have God? But there is no reason either why we should waste our time in weighing the respective merits of the gods of Spinoza, of Leibniz, or of Descartes. We now know what these gods are: mere by-products born of the philosophical decomposition of the Christian living God. Today our only choice is not Kant or Descartes; it is rather Kant or Thomas Aquinas. All the other positions are but halfway houses on the roads which lead either to absolute religious agnosticism or to the natural theology of Christian metaphysics.[4]

Philosophical halfway houses have always been pretty crowded, but never more than they are in our own times, especially in the field of natural theology. This fact is not a wholly inexplicable one. What makes it difficult for us to go back to Thomas Aquinas is Kant. Modern men are held spellbound by science, in some cases because they know it, but in an incomparably larger number of cases because

4. Cf. the philosophical manifesto of Rudolf Eucken, *Thomas von Aquino und Kant, ein Kampf zweier Welten* (Berlin, Reuther and Richard, 1901).

they know that, to those who know science, the problem of God does not appear susceptible of a scientific formulation. But what makes it difficult for us to go as far as Kant is, if not Thomas Aquinas himself, at least the whole order of facts which provides a basis for his own natural theology. Quite apart from any philosophical demonstration of the existence of God, there is such a thing as a spontaneous natural theology. A quasi-instinctive tendency, observable in most men, seems to invite them to wonder from time to time if, after all, there is not such an unseen being as the one we call God. The current objection that such a feeling is but a survival in us of primitive myths, or of our own early religious education, is not a very strong one. Primitive myths do not account for the human belief in the existence of the Divinity; obviously, it is the reverse which is true. Early religious education is no sufficient explanation for the questions which sometimes arise in the minds of men concerning the reality or unreality of God. Some among us have received a decidedly antireligious education; others have had no religious education at all; and there are even quite a few who, having once received a religious education, fail to find in its memory any incentive to think too seriously of God.[5] The natural invitations to apply his mind to the problem come to man from quite different sources. These are the very selfsame sources which once gave rise not only to Greek mythology but to all mythologies. God spontaneously offers himself to most of us, more as a confusedly felt presence than as an answer to any problem, when we find ourselves confronted with the vastness of the ocean, the still purity of mountains, or the mysterious life of a midsummer starry sky. Far from being social in essence, these fleeting temptations to think of God usually visit us in our moments of solitude. But there is no more solitary solitude than that of a man in deep sorrow or confronted with the tragic perspective of his own impending end. "One dies alone," Pascal says. That is perhaps the reason why so many men finally meet God waiting for them on the threshold of death.

What do such feelings prove? Absolutely nothing. They are not proofs but facts, the very facts which give philosophers occasion to ask themselves precise questions concerning the possible existence of God. Just as such

5. Knowing the temptations to which historians sometimes succumb, I deem it safer to specify that there is nothing autobiographical in this last remark.

personal experiences precede any attempt to prove that there is a God, they survive our failures to prove it. Pascal did not make much of the so-called proofs of God's existence. To him, it was incomprehensible that God should exist, and it was incomprehensible that God should not exist; then he would simply wager that God exist—a safe betting indeed, since there was much to gain and nothing to lose. Thus to bet is not to know, especially in a case when, if we lose, we cannot even hope to know it. Yet Pascal was still willing to bet on what he could not know. Similarly, after proving in his *Critique of Pure Reason* that the existence of God could not be demonstrated, Kant still insisted on keeping God as at least a unifying idea in the order of speculative reason and as postulate in the moral order of practical reason. It may even appear to be true that, out of its own nature, the human mind is equally unable both to prove the existence of any God and "to escape its deep-seated instinct to personify its intellectual conceptions."[6] Whether we make it the result of spontaneous judgment of reason, with Thomas

6. Thomas Henry Huxley, *The Evolution of Theology: an Anthropological Study,* as quoted in Julian Huxley, *Essays in Popular Science* (London, Pelican Books, 1937), p. 123.

Aquinas; or an innate idea, with Descartes; or an intellectual intuition, with Malebranche; or an idea born of the unifying power of human reason, with Kant; or a phantasm of human imagination, with Thomas Henry Huxley, this common notion of God is there as a practically universal fact whose speculative value may well be disputed, but whose existence cannot be denied. The only problem is for us to determine the truth value of this notion.

At first sight, the shortest way to test it seems to judge it from the point of view of scientific knowledge. But the shortest way might not be the safest one. This method rests upon the assumption that nothing can be rationally known unless it be scientifically known, which is far from being an evident proposition. The names of Kant and of Comte have very little importance, if any, in the history of modern science; Descartes and Leibniz, two of the creators of modern science, have also been great metaphysicians. The simple truth may be that while human reason remains one and the same in dealing with different orders of problems, it nevertheless must approach these various orders of problems in as many different ways. Whatever our final answer to the problem of God may be, we all agree that God is not an empirically observable fact. Mystical experience itself is both unspeakable and intransmissible; hence, it cannot become an objective experience. If, speaking in the order of pure natural knowledge, the proposition "God exists" makes any sense at all, it must be for its rational value as a philosophical answer to a metaphysical question.

When a man falls to wondering whether there is such a being as God, he is not conscious of raising a scientific problem, or hoping to give it a scientific solution. Scientific problems are all related to the knowledge of *what* given things actually are. An ideal scientific explanation of the world would be an exhaustive rational explanation of *what* the world actually is; but *why* nature exists is not a scientific problem, because its answer is not susceptible of empirical verification. The notion of God, on the contrary, always appears to us in history as an answer to some existential problem, that is, as the *why* of a certain existence. The Greek gods were constantly invoked in order to account for various "happenings" in the history of men as well as in that of things. A religious interpretation of nature never worries about what things are—that is a problem for scientists—but it is very much concerned with the questions why things happen to be precisely what they are, and why they happen to be at all. The Jewish-Christian God to whom we are introduced by the Bible is there at once posited as the ultimate explanation for the very existence of man, for the present condition of man upon earth, for all the successive events that make up the history of the Jewish people as well as for these momentous events: the Incarnation of Christ and the Redemption of man by Grace. Whatever their ultimate value, these are existential answers to existential questions. As such, they cannot possibly be transposed into terms of science, but only into terms of an existential metaphysics. Hence these two immediate consequences: that natural theology is in bondage not to the method of positive science but to the method of metaphysics, and that it can correctly ask its own problems only in the frame of an existential metaphysics.

Of these two conclusions, the first one is doomed to remain very unpopular. To tell the whole truth, it sounds perfectly absurd to say, and ridiculous to maintain, that the highest metaphysical problems in no way depend upon the answers given by science to its own questions. The most common view of this matter is best expressed by these words of a modern astronomer: "Before the philosophers have a right to speak, science ought first to be asked to tell all she can as to ascertain facts and provisional hypotheses. Then, and then only, may discussion legitimately pass into the realms of philosophy."[7] This, I quite agree, looks much more sensible than what I myself have said. But when people behave as if what I have said were false, what does happen? In 1696, John Toland decided to discuss religious problems by a method borrowed from natural philosophy. The result was his book, which I have already mentioned: *Christianity Not Mysterious*. Now, if Christianity

7. Sir James Jeans, *The Mysterious Universe* (London, Pelican Books, 1937), Foreword, p. vii. The relation of philosophy to science is curiously misunderstood by some scientists. It is true that "few in this age would willingly base their lives on a philosophy which to the man of science is demonstrably false." But it does not follow that "science thus takes the place of the foundation on which the structure of our lives must be built if we wish that structure to be stable." Arthur H. Compton, *The Religion of a Scientist* (New York, The Jewish Theological Seminary of America, 1938), p. 5. First of all, science itself is not stable. Secondly, from the fact that no set of propositions can be held as true if it contradicts another set of propositions that are demonstrably true, it does not follow that this second set of propositions must provide the foundation whereupon to establish our lives. It is quite possible, for instance, that the philosophical propositions whereupon we must establish our lives are quite independent of all conceivable sets of scientific propositions.

is not mysterious, what is? In 1930, in his Rede Lecture delivered before the University of Cambridge, Sir James Jeans decided to deal with philosophical problems in the light of contemporary science. The upshot was his most popular book: *The Mysterious Universe.* Now, if the universe of science is mysterious, what is not? We do not need science to tell us that the universe is indeed mysterious. Men have known that since the very beginning of the human race. The true and proper function of science is, on the contrary, to make as much of the universe as possible grow less and less mysterious to us. Science does it, and she does it magnificently. Any sixteen-year-old boy, in any one of our schools, knows more today about the physical structure of the world than Thomas Aquinas, Aristotle, or Plato ever did. He can give rational explanations of phenomena which once appeared to the greatest minds as puzzling mysteries. The universe of science *qua* science exactly consists of that part of the total universe from which, owing to human reason, mysteries have been removed.

How is it, then, that a scientist can feel well founded in calling this universe a "mysterious universe"? Is it because the very progress of science brings him face to face with phenomena that are more and more difficult to observe and whose laws are more and more difficult to formulate? But the unknown is not necessarily a mystery; and science naturally proceeds upon the assumption that it is not, because it is at least knowable, even though we do not yet know it. The true reason why this universe appears to some scientists as mysterious is that, mistaking existential, that is, metaphysical, questions for scientific ones, they ask science to answer them. Naturally, they get no answers. Then they are puzzled, and they say that the universe is mysterious.

The scientific cosmogony of Sir James Jeans himself exhibits an instructive collection of such perplexities. His starting point is the actual existence of innumerable stars "wandering about space" at such enormous distances from one another "that it is an event of almost unimaginable rarity for a star to come anywhere near to another star." Yet, we must "believe" that "some two thousand million years ago, this rare event took place, and that a second star, wandering blindly through space," happened to come so near the sun that it raised a huge tidal wave on its surface. This mountainous wave finally exploded, and its fragments, still "circulating around their parent sun . . . are the planets, great and small, of which our earth is one." These ejected fragments of the sun gradually cooled; "in course of time, we know not how, when, or why, one of these cooling fragments gave birth to life." Hence, the emergence of a stream of life which has culminated in man. In a universe where empty space is deadly cold and most of the matter deadly hot, the emergence of life was highly improbable. Nevertheless, "into such a universe we have stumbled, if not exactly by mistake, at least as the result of what may properly be described as an accident." Such is, Sir James Jeans concludes, "the surprising manner in which, so far as science can at present inform us, we came into being."[8]

That all this is very mysterious everybody will agree, but the question then arises: Is this science? Even if we take them, as their author evidently does, for so many "provisional hypotheses," can we consider such hypotheses as being, in any sense of the word, scientific? Is it scientific to explain the existence of man by a series of accidents, each of which is more improbable than the other one? The truth of the case simply is that on the problem of the existence of man modern astronomy has strictly nothing to say. And the same conclusion holds good if, to modern astronomy, we add modern

8. Sir James Jeans, *op. cit.*, chap. i, pp. 11–22.

physics. When, after describing the physical world of Einstein, Heisenberg, Dirac, Lemaître, and Louis de Broglie, he at last takes a dive into what, this time at least, he knows to be "the deep waters" of metaphysics, what conclusion does Sir James Jeans ultimately reach? That although many scientists prefer the notion of a "cyclic universe, the more orthodox scientific view" is that this universe owes its present form to a "creation" and that "its creation must have been an act of thought."[9] Granted. But what have these answers to do with Einstein, Heisenberg, and the justly famous galaxy of modern physicists? The two doctrines of a "cyclical universe" and of a supreme Thought were formulated by pre-Socratic philosophers who knew nothing of what Einstein would say twenty-six centuries after them. "Modern scientific theory," Jeans adds, "compels us to think of the creator as working outside time and space, which are part of his creation, just as the artist is outside his canvas."[10] Why should modern theory compel us to say what has already been said, not only by Saint Augustine, whom our scientist quotes, but by any and every one of countless Christian theologians who knew no

9. *Ibid.*, chap. v, p. 182.
10. *Ibid.*, chap. v, p. 183.

other world than that of Ptolemy? Clearly enough, the philosophical answer of Sir James Jeans to the problem of the world order has absolutely nothing to do with modern science. And no wonder, since it has absolutely nothing to do with any scientific knowledge at all.

If we consider it more closely, the initial question asked by Jeans had taken him at once not only into deep waters but, scientifically speaking, out of soundings. To ask the question why, out of an infinity of possible combinations of physicochemical elements, there has arisen the living and thinking being we call man is to seek the cause why such a complex of physical energies as man actually is, or exists. In other words, it is to inquire into the possible causes for the *existence* of living and thinking organisms upon earth. The hypothesis that living substances may tomorrow be produced by biochemists in their laboratories is irrelevant to the question. If a chemist ever succeeds in turning out living cells, or some elementary sorts of organisms, nothing will be easier for him than to say why such organisms exist. His answer will be: I made them. Our own question is not at all: Are living and thinking beings made up of nothing else than physical elements? It rather is: Supposing they ultimately consist of nothing else, how can we account for the *existence* of the very order of molecules which produces what we call life, and thought?

Scientifically speaking, such problems do not make sense. If there were no living and thinking beings, there would be no science. Hence there would be no questions. Even the scientific universe of inorganic matter is a structural universe; as to the world of organic matter, it everywhere exhibits coördination, adaptation, functions. When asked why there are such organized beings, scientists answer: Chance. Now anybody may fluke a brilliant stroke at billiards; but when a billiard player makes a run of a hundred, to say that he fluked it is to offer a rather weak explanation. Some scientists know this so well that they substitute for the notion of chance the notion of mechanical laws, which is its very reverse. But when they come to explaining how these mechanical laws have given rise to living organized beings, they are driven back to chance as to the last reason it is possible to quote. "The powers operating in the cosmos," Julian Huxley says, "are, though unitary, yet subdivisible; and, though subdivisible, yet related. There are the vast powers of inorganic nature, neutral or hostile to man. Yet they gave birth to evolving life, whose development, though blind and fortuitous, has tended in the same general direction as our own conscious desires and ideals, and so gives us an external sanction for our directional activities. This again gave birth to human mind, which, in the race, is changing the course of evolution by acceleration,"[11] and so on, ad infinitum. In other words, the only scientific reasons why our billiard player makes a run of a hundred are that he cannot play billiards and that all the chances are against it.

If scientists, speaking as scientists, have no intelligible answer to this problem, why are some of them so keen on talking nonsense about it? The reason is simple, and this time we can be sure that chance has nothing to do with their obstinacy. They prefer to say anything rather than to ascribe existence to God on the ground that a purpose exists in the universe. Now there is some justification for their attitude. Just as science can play havoc with metaphysics, metaphysics can play havoc with science. Coming before science in the past, it has often done so to the point of pre-

11. Julian Huxley, "Rationalism and the Idea of God," in *Essays of a Biologist,* chap. vi (London, Pelican Books, 1939), p. 176. This "scientific" cosmogony strangely resembles the *Theogony* of Hesiod, where everything is successively begotten from original Chaos.

venting its rise and of blocking its development. For centuries final causes have been mistaken for scientific explanations by so many generations of philosophers that today many scientists still consider the fear of final causes as the beginning of scientific wisdom. Science is thus making metaphysics suffer for its centuries-long meddling in matters of physics and biology.

In both cases, however, the real victim of this epistemological strife is one and the same: the human mind. Nobody denies that living organisms appear as though they had been designed, or intended, to fulfill the various functions related to life. Everybody agrees that this appearance may be but an illusion. We would be bound to hold it for an illusion if science could account for the rise of life by its usual explanations of mechanical type, where nothing more is involved than the relations of observable phenomena according to the geometrical properties of space and the physical laws of motion. What is most remarkable, on the contrary, is that many scientists obstinately maintain the illusory character of this appearance though they freely acknowledge their failure to imagine any scientific explanation for the organic constitution of living beings. As soon as modern physics had reached the structural problems raised by molecular physics, it found itself confronted with such difficulties. Yet scientists much preferred to introduce into physics the nonmechanical notions of discontinuity and indeterminacy rather than resort to anything like design. On a much larger scale, we have seen Julian Huxley boldly account for the existence of organized bodies by those very properties of matter which, according to himself, make it infinitely improbable that such bodies should ever exist. Why should those eminently rational beings, the scientists, deliberately prefer to the simple notions of design, or purposiveness, in nature, the arbitrary notions of blind force, chance, emergence, sudden variation, and similar ones? Simply because they much prefer a complete absence of intelligibility to the presence of a nonscientific intelligibility.

We seem to be here reaching at last the very core of this epistemological problem. Unintelligible as they are, these arbitrary notions are at least homogeneous with a chain of mechanical interpretations. Posited at the beginning of such a chain, or inserted in it where they are needed, they provide the scientist with the very existences which he needs in order to have something to know.

Their very irrationality is expressive of the invincible resistance opposed by existence to any type of scientific explanation.[12] By accepting design, or purposiveness, as a possible principle of explanation, a scientist would introduce into his system of laws a ring wholly heterogeneous with the rest of the chain. He would intertwine the metaphysical causes for the existence of organisms with the physical causes which he must assign to both their structure and their functioning. Still worse, he might feel tempted to mistake the existential causes of living organisms for their efficient and physical causes, thus coming back to the good old times when fishes had fins because they had been made to swim. Now it may well be true that fishes have been made to swim, but when we know it we know just as much about fishes as we know about airplanes when we know that they are made to fly. If they had not been made to fly, there would be no airplanes, since to be flying-machines is their very definition; but it takes us at least two

12. The marked antipathy of modern science toward the notion of efficient cause is intimately related to the nonexistential character of scientific explanations. It is of the essence of an efficient cause that it makes something be, or exist. Since the relation of effect to cause is an existential and a nonanalytical one, it appears to the scientific mind as a sort of scandal which must be eliminated.

sciences, aerodynamics and mechanics, in order to know how they do fly. A final cause has posited an existence whose science alone can posit the laws.

This heterogeneity of these two orders was strikingly expressed by Francis Bacon, when he said, speaking of final causes, that "in physics, they are impertinent, and as remoras to the ship, that hinder the sciences from holding their course of improvement."[13] Their scientific sterility is particularly complete in a world like that of modern science, where essences have been reduced to mere phenomena, themselves reduced to the order of that which can be observed. Modern scientists live, or they pretend to live, in a world of mere appearances, where that which appears is the appearance of nothing. Yet the fact that final causes are scientifically sterile does not entail their disqualification as metaphysical causes, and to reject metaphysical answers to a problem just because they are not scientific is deliberately to maim the knowing power of the

13. Francis Bacon, *The Dignity and Advancement of Learning,* Bk. III, chap. iv, ed. J. E. Creighton (New York, The Colonial Press, 1900), p. 97. Cf. p. 98: "These final causes, however, are not false, or unworthy of inquiry in metaphysics, but their excursion into the limits of physical causes has made a great devastation in that province."

human mind. If the only intelligible way to explain the existence of organized bodies is to admit that there is design, purposiveness, at their origin, then let us admit it, if not as scientists, at least as metaphysicians. And since the notions of design and of purpose are for us inseparable from the notion of thought, to posit the existence of a thought as cause of the purposiveness of organized bodies is also to posit an end of all ends, or an ultimate end, that is, God.

It goes without saying that this is the very consequence which the adversaries of final causes intend to deny. "Purpose," Julian Huxley says, "is a psychological term; and to ascribe purpose to a process merely because its results are somewhat similar to those of a true purposeful process is completely unjustified, and a mere projection of our own ideas into the economy of nature."[14] This is most certainly what we do, but why should we not do so? We do not need to *project* our own ideas into the economy of nature; they belong there in their own right. Our own ideas are in the economy of nature because we ourselves are in it. Any and every one of the things which a man does intelligently is done with a purpose and to a certain end which is the final

14. Julian Huxley, *op. cit.*, chap. vi, p. 173.

cause why he does it. Whatever a worker, an engineer, an industrialist, a writer, or an artist makes is but the actualization, by intelligently selected means, of a certain end. There is no known example of a self-made machine spontaneously arising in virtue of the mechanical laws of matter. Through man, who is part and parcel of nature, purposiveness most certainly is part and parcel of nature. In what sense then is it arbitrary, knowing from within that where there is organization there always is a purpose, to conclude that there is a purpose wherever there is organization? I fully understand a scientist who turns down such an inference as wholly nonscientific. I also understand a scientist who tells me that, as a scientist, he has no business to draw any inference as to the possible cause why organized bodies actually exist. But I wholly fail to see in what sense my inference, if I choose to draw it, is "a common fallacy."

Why should there be a fallacy in inferring that there is purpose in the universe on the ground of biological progress? Because, Julian Huxley answers, this "can be shown to be as natural and inevitable a product of the struggle for existence as is adaptation, and to be no more mysterious than, for instance, the increase in effectiveness both of armour-piercing projectile and armour-plate during the last century."[15] Does Julian Huxley suggest that steel plates have spontaneously grown thicker as shells were growing heavier during the last century? In other words, does he maintain that purposiveness is as wholly absent from human industry as it is from the rest of the world? Or does he perhaps maintain that the rest of the world is as full of purposiveness as human industry obviously is? In the name of science he maintains both, namely, that adaptations in organisms are no more mysterious where there is no purposiveness to account for them, than is adaptation in human industry where purposiveness everywhere accounts for it. That adaptations due to a purpose*less* struggle for life are no more mysterious than adaptations due to a purpose*ful* struggle—whether this proposition is "a common fallacy," I do not know, but it certainly seems to be a fallacy. It is the fallacy of a scientist who, because he does not know how to ask metaphysical problems, obstinately refuses their correct metaphysical answers. In the *Inferno* of the world of knowledge, there is a special punishment for this sort of sin; it is the relapse into mythology. Better known as a distinguished zoologist, Julian Huxley

15. *Ibid.*, p. 172.

must also be credited with having added the god Struggle to the already large family of the Olympians.[16]

A world which has lost the Christian God cannot but resemble a world which had not yet found him. Just like the world of Thales and of Plato, our own modern world is "full of gods." There are blind Evolution, clear-sighted Orthogenesis, benevolent Progress, and others which it is more advisable not to mention by name. Why unnecessarily hurt the feelings of men who, today, render them a cult? It is however important for us to realize that mankind is doomed to live more and more under the spell of a new scientific, social, and political mythology, unless we resolutely exorcise these befuddled notions whose influence on modern life is becoming appalling. Millions of men are starving and bleeding to death because two or three of these pseudoscientific or pseudosocial deified abstractions are now at war. For when gods fight among themselves, men have to die. Could we not make an effort to realize that evolution is to be largely what we will make it to be? That

16. On the philosophical difficulties entailed by this notion of evolution, see W. R. Thompson, *Science and Common Sense,* pp. 216–232.

Progress is not an automatically self-achieving law but something to be patiently achieved by the will of men? That Equality is not an actually given fact but an ideal to be progressively approached by means of justice? That Democracy is not the leading goddess of some societies but a magnificent promise to be fulfilled by all through their obstinate will for friendship, if they are strong enough to make it last for generations after generations?

I think we could, but a good deal of clear thinking should come first, and this is where, in spite of its proverbial helplessness, philosophy might be of some help. The trouble with so many of our contemporaries is not that they are agnostics but rather that they are misguided theologians. Real agnostics are exceedingly rare, and they harm nobody but themselves. Just as they have no God, these have no gods. Much more common, unfortunately, are those pseudo-agnostics who, because they combine scientific knowledge and social generosity with a complete lack of philosophical culture, substitute dangerous mythologies for the natural theology which they do not even understand.

The problem of final causes is perhaps the problem most commonly discussed by these modern agnostics. As such, it particularly recommended itself to our attention. It is nevertheless only one among the many aspects of the highest of all metaphysical problems, that of Being. Beyond the question: Why are there organized beings? lies this deeper one, which I am asking in Leibniz's own terms: Why is there something rather than nothing? Here again, I fully understand a scientist who refuses to ask it. He is welcome to tell me that the question does not make sense. Scientifically speaking, it does not.[17] Metaphysi-

17. The hostility exhibited by a wholly mathematized science toward the irreducible act of existence is what lies behind its opposition, so well marked by H. Bergson, to duration itself. Malebranche considered the existence of matter as indemonstrable; hence his conclusion that the annihilation of the material world by God would in no way affect our scientific knowledge of it. Sir Arthur Eddington would certainly not subscribe to Malebranche's metaphysics; but his own approach to the problem of existence is an epistemological one, namely, this particular body of knowledge which we call modern physics; hence the analogous consequence that, from such a point of view, "the question of attributing a mysterious property called *existence* to the physical universe never arises." *The Philosophy of Physical Science* (Cambridge, University Press, 1939), chap. x, pp. 156–157. As a substitute for the "metaphysical concept of *real existence,*" Sir Arthur offers a "structural concept of existence," which he defines in pp. 162–166. In point of fact, there is a metaphysical concept of *being,* which is not "hazy" (p. 162), but analogical; as to actual existence, it is not an object of concept, but of judgment. To substitute "struc-

cally speaking, however, it does. Science can account for many things in the world; it may some day account for all that which the world of phenomena actually is. But why anything at all is, or exists, science knows not, precisely because it cannot even ask the question.

To this supreme question, the only conceivable answer is that each and every particular existential energy, each and every particular existing thing, depends for its existence upon a pure Act of existence.[18] In order

tural existence" for "real existence" is to be headed for the conclusion that "independent existence" is, for a given element, "its existence as a contributor to the structure," whereas its nonexistence is "a hole occurring in, or added to, the structure" (p. 165). In other words, the *independent* existence, or nonexistence, of an element is strictly dependent upon its whole. To exist is "to be a-contributor-to"; to cease to exist is to cease "to be a-contributor-to." Yet, in order to be a contributor to some whole, a thing has first to be; and to define the death of a man by the hole it creates in his family is to take a rather detached view of what appears to the dying man himself as an intensely individuated event.

18. Sir Arthur Eddington complains that philosophers do nothing to make clear to "laymen" what the word "existence" means. *The Philosophy of Physical Science,* chap. x, pp. 154–157. As an example of its ambiguity, Sir Arthur quotes the judgment: There is an overdraft at the bank. Is an "overdraft at a bank" something that exists? The answer is: Yes, and no. The verbal form "is" has two distinct meanings, according as it designates: (1) the actual existence of a thing; (2) the composition of a predicate with a subject in a judgment. What exists at

to be the ultimate answer to all existential problems, this supreme cause has to be absolute existence.[19] Being absolute, such a cause is self-sufficient; if it creates, its creative act must be free. Since it creates not only being but order, it must be something which at least eminently contains the only principle of order known to us in experience, namely, thought. Now an absolute, self-subsisting, and knowing cause is not an It but a He. In short, the first

the bank, in sense number one, is a draft; but it is true, in sense number two, that "this draft is an overdraft." To say that "a draft is an overdraft," is by no means to say that an "overdraft" actually is, or exists.

19. Some scientists, who still realize the value of the argument on the basis of design, would say that they do not feel "the need of a Creator to start the Universe." A. H. Compton, *The Religion of a Scientist,* p. 11. In other words, they do not realize that these two problems are identically the same. Design appears to them as a fact whose *existence* calls for an explanation. Why then should not the protons, electrons, neutrons, and photons be considered as facts whose *existence* also calls for some explanation? In what sense is the existence of these elements less mysterious than that of their composite? What prevents many scientists from going as far as to ask this second question is that, this time, they cannot fail to perceive the nonscientific character of the problem. Yet the nature of the two problems is the same. If the cause for the *existence* of organisms lies outside the nature of their physicochemical elements, it transcends the physical order; hence it is transphysical, that is, metaphysical, in its own right. In other words, if there is nothing in the elements to account for design, the presence of design in a chaos of elements entails just as necessarily a *creation* as the very existence of the elements.

cause is the One in whom the cause of both nature and history coincide, a philosophical God who can also be the God of a religion.[20]

To go one step further would be to match the mistake of some agnostics with a similar one. The failure of too many metaphysicians to distinguish between philosophy and religion has proved no less harmful to natural theology than have the encroachments of pseudometaphysical science. Metaphysics pos-

20. Dr. A. H. Compton is an interesting instance of those many scientists who do not seem to be aware of crossing any border lines when they pass from science to philosophy and from philosophy to religion. To them the "hypothesis God" is just one more of those "working hypotheses" which a scientist provisorily accepts as true in spite of the fact that none of them can be proved. Hence the consequence that "faith in God may be a thoroughly scientific attitude, even though we may be unable to establish the correctness of our belief." *The Religion of a Scientist,* p. 13. This is a regrettable confusion of language. It is true the principle of the conservation of energy and the notion of evolution are hypotheses; but they are *scientific* hypotheses because, according as we accept or reject them, our scientific interpretation of observable facts is bound to become different. The existence or nonexistence of God, on the contrary, is a proposition whose negation or affirmation determines no change whatever in the structure of our scientific explanation of the world and is wholly independent of the contents of science as such. Supposing, for instance, there be design in the world, the existence of God cannot be posited as a *scientific* explanation for the presence of design in the world; it is a *metaphysical* one; consequently, God has not to be posited as a *scientific probability* but as a *metaphysical necessity.*

its God as a pure Act of existence, but it does not provide us with any concept of His essence. We know that He is; we do not comprehend Him. Simple-minded metaphysicians have unwillingly led agnostics to believe that the God of natural theology was the "watchmaker" of Voltaire, or the "carpenter" of cheap apologetics. First of all, no watch has ever been made by any watchmaker; "watchmakers" as such simply do not exist; watches are made by men who know how to make watches. Similarly, to posit God as the supreme cause of that which is, is to know that He is He who can create, because He is "He who is"; but this tells us still less concerning what absolute existence can be than any piece of carpentry tells us about the man who made it. Being men, we can affirm God only on anthropomorphic grounds, but this does not oblige us to posit Him as an anthropomorphic God. As Saint Thomas Aquinas says:

> The verb *to be* is used in two different ways: in a first one, it signifies the act of existing (*actu essendi*); in the second one it signifies the composition of those propositions which the soul invents by joining a predicate with a subject. Taking *to be* in the first way, we cannot know the "to be" of God (*esse Dei*), no more than we know His essence. We know it in the

second way only. For, indeed, we know that the proposition we are forming about God, when we say: God is, is a true proposition, and we know this from His effects.[21]

If such be the God of natural theology, true metaphysics does not culminate in a concept, be it that of Thought, of Good, of One, or of Substance. It does not even culminate in an essence, be it that of Being itself. Its last word is not *ens*, but *esse;* not *being*, but *is*. The ultimate effort of true metaphysics is to posit an Act by an act, that is, to posit by an act of judging the supreme Act of existing whose very essence, because it is to be, passes human understanding. Where a man's metaphysics comes to an end, his religion begins. But the only path which can lead him to the point where the true religion begins must of necessity lead him beyond the contemplation of essences, up to the very mystery of existence. This path is not very hard to find, but few are those who dare to follow it to the end. Seduced as they are by the intelligible beauty of science, many men lose all taste for metaphysics and religion. A few others, absorbed in the contemplation of some supreme cause, become aware that metaphysics and religion

21. Saint Thomas Aquinas, *Summa theologica,* Pars I, qu. 3, art. 4, ad 2^{m}.

should ultimately meet, but they cannot tell how or where; hence they separate religion from philosophy, or else they renounce religion for philosophy, if they do not, like Pascal, renounce philosophy for religion. Why should not we keep truth, and keep it whole? It can be done. But only those can do it who realize that He Who is the God of the philosophers is HE WHO IS, the God of Abraham, of Isaac, and of Jacob.

INDEX

Alfaric, P., 44 n.
Anaximander, 4
Anaximenes, 4, 13
Aristotle, ix, 1, 2, 14–15 n., 32–34, 43–44, 45, 47, 62, 66–67, 85, 105, 110, 122
Augustine, Saint, 44–45, 47–49, 53–62, 72–73, 91, 92, 97, 110

Bacon, Francis, 132
Bergson, H., xii–xiii, 138 n.
Berkeley, G., 74
Blondel, M., 88 n.
Blount, Charles, 106
Bossuet, J. B., 104
Boyer, Charles, 44 n.
de Broglie, Louis, 125
Brunschvicg, L., 113
Burnet, John, 3–5, 14–15 n.

Chapman, Emmanuel, 61 n.
Cicero, 2 n.
Compton, Arthur H., 121 n., 140 n., 141 n.
Comte, A., 109–115, 118
Condillac, 74
Cornford, F. M., 4 n.
de Corte, Marcel, 57 n.
Cousin, V., 80–81 n.

Deists, 104–108
Delbos, V., 100 n.
Demokritus, 17–18
Descartes, R., xiii–xiv, 74–91, 92–98, 100, 110–111, 114, 118
Dies, A., 18 n., 26 n.
Dirac, 125
Dryden, J., 105
Duns Scotus, 68–69
Durkheim, É., 113

Eddington, Sir Arthur, 138–139 n., 139–140 n.
Einstein, A., 125
Epicurus, 35
Espinas, A., 80–81
Eucken, R., 114 n.

Festugière, A. J., 7 n., 25–26 n., 35 n.
Fontenelle, 107
Frischeisen-Köhler, Max, 105 n.

Gardeil, A., 61 n., 64–65 n.
Gilson, É., autobiographical, xii–xv, 116; references to his other works, ix, xiii, 42 n., 56 n., 61 n., 63 n., 64 n., 80 n., 85 n., 109 n.
God, Christian, 38–44; Jewish, 38–44
Gods, Greek, 1–23, 41
Gouhier, H., 80–81 n., 92 n.

Hack, R. K., 2 n., 6 n., 7 n., 14–15 n., 17 n., 23 n.
Hamelin, O., 78
Heisenberg, W., 125
Herbert of Cherbury, 106

Hesiod, 5–6, 17 n., 23 n., 31 n., 128 n.
Homer, 5–17, 23 n., 29, 31 n., 32, 41
Hortatory Address to the Greeks, 42
Huxley, Julian, 127-128, 130, 133–136
Huxley, T. H., 117 n., 118

Jeans, Sir James, 121 n., 122, 123–128
Jehovah, 40
John Damascene, 63 n.
John, Saint, 48, 55
Justin Martyr, 42 n.

Kant, I., 109–115, 117, 118

Leibniz, 98–100, 110–111, 114, 118, 138
Lemaître, J., 125
Lévy-Bruhl, L., xiii, 80–81 n.
Liard, L., 80–81
Littré, É., 113
Locke, J., 110–111

Malebranche, 74, 88 n., 91–98, 110–111, 118, 138 n.
Marcus Aurelius, 35–36, 102
Maritain, J., xv, 65 n., 76 n., 113 n.
Mass, The Ordinary of the, 58 n.
Meyer, Edward, 6 n.
Meyerson, É., 111 n.
Mill, J. S., 113
Minges, Parthenius, 69 n.
Moog, Willy, 105 n.
Moses, 38–44, 67, 91–92
Muller-Thym, J. B., 44
Murray, Gilbert, 6 n., 7 n., 62

Newton, I., 107, 109, 111
Novalis, 102 n.

Olgiati, F., 80–81 n.

Pascal, B., 88 n., 90, 116–117, 144
Paulsen, F., 113
Pegis, Anton C., 64–65 n.
Philosophy, Christian, xvii, 42–43; contemporary, xiv–xv; Greek, 42–43; historical approach to, ix–xii; medieval, 74; modern, 74
Pindar, 12
Plato, ix, 23–32, 34, 42–44, 45, 47, 54–63, 82, 97, 102, 105, 107, 122, 136
Plotinos, 44–47, 48–51, 53–60, 93, 97

Religion, Greek, 1–23; Jewish, 38–44
Renouvier, C., 113
Revelation, Jewish-Christian, 38–44
Robespierre, 106
Robin, L., 23 n.
Rohde, E., 6 n.
Rosmini, G., 74
Rousseau, J., 106, 107

Spencer, H., 113
Spinoza, B., 100–105, 107, 110–111, 114
Stoics, 2 n., 14, 35–37, 45

Thales, 1–6, 13, 14–15 n., 29, 30, 136
Thomas Aquinas, Saint, xi–xiv, xvi, 58 n., 62–73, 75–77, 84–90, 92, 96, 110, 114–115, 117–118, 122, 142–143
Thompson, W. R., 113 n., 136 n.
Tindal, Matthew, 106
Toland, John, 106, 121

Vaihinger, H., 113
Viret, P., 105 n.
Voltaire, 99, 106, 107, 142

Wilamowitz, U. v., 6 n.

Yahweh, 40

Note. References other than those to proper names are incomplete. They are included as a guide to important sections not indicated by proper name references.